The Color of Water:
A Black Man's Tribute to
His White Mother

James McBride

Curriculum Unit

Tami J. Strege

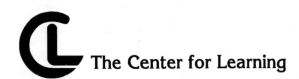
The Center for Learning

Tami J. Strege, who earned her M.A. in multicultural education from Prescott College, Arizona, has been published in the *English Journal*. She coauthored The Center for Learning novel/drama curriculum units *Shabanu: Daughter of the Wind/Haveli, Farewell to Manzanar/Black Like Me,* and *Year of Impossible Goodbyes/So Far from the Bamboo Grove.* She is also the author of the novel/drama unit *Snow Falling on Cedars.*

The Publishing Team

Rose Schaffer, M.A., President/Chief Executive Officer
Bernadette Vetter, M.A., Vice President
Diana Culbertson, Ph.D., Editor

Cover Design

Susan Chowanetz Thornton, B.S.

List of credits found on Acknowledgments page
beginning on 73.

ISBN 1-56077-600-5

Contents

Introduction

"The main thing is to make history, not to write it." Otto von Bismarck would certainly agree that Ruth McBride Jordan, the main character of James McBride's *The Color of Water: A Black Man's Tribute to His White Mother*, has made history. Her story—and the author's, her son—is a remarkable success story, a testimony to her strength of spirit, secure and sound values, and unconquerable will.

The Color of Water tells the true story of Ruth McBride Jordan, the two kind and remarkable men she married, and the twelve outstanding children she raised, largely by herself. Jordan, born Rachel Shilsky, a Polish Jew, immigrated to America as a child; as a young adult she left her family and Judaism behind in Virginia and moved to New York City. There she met and married a black man, a decision that further increased her isolation.

Ruth McBride Jordan combated racism and, at times, nearly crippling poverty to raise her children, but her strength of spirit never faltered. H. Jack Geiger of the *New York Times Book Review* wrote that "the triumph of the book—and of their lives—is that race and religion are transcended by family love."

The Color of Water, taking the form of a memoir, speaks to the truth that our lives can be illuminated through oral histories that show often incomprehensible historic events in a more intimate, more personal, more realistic light. It has been argued that textbook history is too often a predigested, synthetic version of the past, devoid of humanity and flesh-and-blood reality. Oral history, however, makes the past come alive.

The Color of Water affords readers the opportunity to examine a myriad of values—among them, faith, tolerance, and responsibility—and to discover how to apply them to their own lives.

Teacher Notes

This unit presents ten lesson plans for *The Color of Water: A Black Man's Tribute to His White Mother* by James McBride. Accompanying each lesson plan are reproducible handouts for both large and small groups, as well as individual use. Each lesson is designed for at least a single class session with additional activities that may be used at the teacher's discretion.

The lessons emphasize the significance of faith and love and examine the importance of education. Furthermore, students will explore the journeys of self-discovery that McBride—and they—must take.

Critical and creative thinking skills are also emphasized throughout the lessons. To promote increased reading comprehension and enjoyment, an effort has been made to address active reading strategies including predicting, questioning, connecting, clarifying, and evaluating. Suggestions for practicing these skills are included in the lesson plans.

These lessons emphasize character development, theme, allusion, and other literary elements. The optional activities present expanded opportunities for students to explore the themes of the narrative.

The edition used for this study is the 1996 paperback publication by Riverhead Books, a division of Penguin Putnam, Inc.

The reading assignments that accompany this curriculum unit are as follows:

Chapters 1–4 for Lesson 3

Chapters 5–8 for Lesson 4

Chapters 9–12 for Lesson 5

Chapters 13–16 for Lesson 6

Chapters 17–20 for Lesson 7

Chapters 21–24 for Lesson 8

Chapter 25 and Epilogue for Lessons 9 and 10

Answers will vary unless otherwise indicated. Students may need additional paper to complete some handouts.

Lesson 1
Learning from the Lives of Others

Objectives

- To examine the genres of memoir and autobiography
- To introduce the literary elements of characterization and allusion

Notes to the Teacher

James McBride uses the genres of memoir and autobiography to tell the remarkable story of his mother, a Polish Jew who fled Europe before World War II, grew up in the South, moved to Harlem as a teenager, married an African American, founded a Baptist church, and saw twelve children through college. Ruth McBride Jordan is all the more inspirational because she was not perfect. Her attitude can be adapted to any person's life or situation.

Lesson 1 uses Frederick Douglass's 1845 autobiography as the basis for activities to introduce literary concepts. It is not coincidental that Douglass espoused many of the beliefs that Ruth McBride Jordan tried to instill in her children.

Procedure

1. Before beginning Lesson 1, assign students to small groups or pairs. Throughout this unit, they should be prepared to move back and forth from small groups to individual work at the teacher's direction.

2. Write the words *memoir, autobiography,* and *biography* on an overhead projector or chalkboard. Ask students to look at the words and to suggest possible definitions. (*Students may note that* memoir *resembles the word* memory; *memoirs focus on the author's personal experiences with historical events or people. Most will define* autobiography *as a story someone tells about him- or herself or what he or she has done, and a* biography *as a story about some real person, as told by someone else.*)

3. Inform students that *The Color of Water: A Black Man's Tribute to His White Mother* is at once a memoir, autobiography, and biography. James McBride joins a long and distinguished line of memoirists and biographers who endeavor to teach us something through the lessons of their own lives and the lives of others.

4. One of America's greatest autobiographers was Frederick Douglass, who escaped from slavery in 1838. He was the most effective abolitionist of his day, inspiring people to fight for the freedom of slaves in the United States. After his supporters purchased his freedom for $750 in 1846, he went on to become an advisor and emissary to Presidents Lincoln, Hayes, and Harrison. His story has been called a triumph of courage and dignity over the brutality of slavery. Point out to students that *The Color of Water* also deals with the courage and dignity of McBride's mother in triumphing over the obstacles in her path.

5. Distribute **Handout 1**. Read this excerpt aloud as a class, pausing to clarify students' questions. Responses to the questions will vary, but they should be supported from the text.

6. Review *metaphor,* a type of figurative language. Students will recall that a metaphor is a comparison of two unlike things that does not use *like* or *as.* Remind students that sometimes writers use ideas as metaphors. For example, a writer hoping to convey patriotic sentiment might refer to the American flag—this symbol of freedom becomes a metaphor for patriotism.

7. Establish that in Douglass's narrative, the "pathway from slavery to freedom" could be seen as a metaphor. Ask students how he was enslaved. (*He was enslaved literally by Mr. Auld, and metaphorically by his inability to read, and thus, to exchange ideas.*)

Guide students to an understanding that, therefore, the "pathway . . . to freedom" Douglass refers to could be a metaphor for his learning to read, a skill that allowed his mind and spirit to be free, even while his body was still enslaved.

8. Distribute **Handout 2**. Discuss with students how people today can be metaphorically enslaved but discover a pathway to freedom. For example, alcoholism and drug abuse enslave the mind, body, and spirit in a metaphorical sense; becoming sober is the pathway to freedom from those addictions.

   Allow students class time to begin this composition. Specify your criteria for a well-written assignment before they begin. Permit students to keep it in a writing portfolio for further refinement as their reading of the book progresses.

9. Review *allusion*, a reference made to a literary work, work of art, or a historical or literary person, place, or event.

   Douglass used an allusion in this selection. As a well-read person, he was familiar with the Bible, and in this passage, used an allusion to *Matthew 25:34–40*.

   Read this text of *Matthew 25:34–40* from the New Revised Standard Version of the Bible:

   > "Then the king will say to those at his right hand, 'Come, you that are blessed by my Father, inherit the kingdom prepared for you from the foundation of the world; for I was hungry and you gave me food, I was thirsty and you gave me something to drink, I was a stranger and you welcomed me, I was naked and you gave me clothing, I was sick and you took care of me, I was in prison and you visited me.' Then the righteous will answer him, 'Lord, when was it that we saw you hungry and gave you food, or thirsty and gave you something to drink? And when was it that we saw you a stranger and welcomed you, or naked and gave you clothing? And when was it that we saw you sick or in prison and visited you?' And the king will answer them, 'Truly I tell you, just as you did it to one of the least of these who are members of my family, you did it to me.'"

10. Instruct students to list the words and phrases from the biblical passage that are similar to the words and phrases Douglass used to describe Mrs. Auld. ("*. . . bread for the hungry, clothes for the naked, . . . comfort for every mourner that came within her reach . . .*")

11. Stress that Douglass wanted to present the true details of his life, events, and people. He tried to show that slavery negatively affected everyone—including slaveholders—corrupting and dehumanizing them, and to prove that African Americans were intelligent human beings, deserving of freedom and education.

    In *The Color of Water*, James McBride also emphasizes that freedom and education were essential in providing dignity to his siblings and himself. Ruth McBride Jordan refused to allow poverty, ignorance, or racism to corrupt and dehumanize her children. She attempted to make learning a priority by parading them "to every free event New York City offered: festivals, zoos, parades, block parties, libraries, concerts."

12. Distribute **Handout 3**. Draw students' attention to part A. Engage students in this exploration of characterization by placing them in pairs to complete this assignment.

13. Provide closure by directing students to part B of **Handout 3**. Include directions for a well-written paragraph.

14. Direct students to look for applications of Douglass's beliefs and exhortations as they begin reading McBride's memoir.

Optional Activities

1. Artistically express your responses to item 3, **Handout 1**. Have your teacher display your creations in the classroom.

2. Read Douglass's narrative in its entirety and prepare a report for the class.

Name _____

Date _____

Telling Stories

Directions: Read this example of autobiography, an excerpt from the *Narrative of the Life of Frederick Douglass, An American Slave.* Answer the questions that follow it.

From Chapter 6

My new mistress proved to be all she appeared when I first met her at the door,—a woman of the kindest heart and finest feelings. She had never had a slave under her control previously to myself, and prior to her marriage she had been dependent upon her own industry for a living. She was by trade a weaver; and by constant application to her business, she had been in a good degree preserved from the blighting and dehumanizing effects of slavery. I was utterly astonished at her goodness. I scarcely knew how to behave towards her. She was entirely unlike any other white woman I had ever seen. I could not approach her as I was accustomed to approach other white ladies. My early instruction was all out of place. The crouching servility, usually so acceptable a quality in a slave, did not answer when manifested toward her. Her favor was not gained by it; she seemed to be disturbed by it. She did not deem it impudent or unmannerly for a slave to look her in the face. The meanest slave was put fully at ease in her presence, and none left without feeling better for having seen her. Her face was made of heavenly smiles, and her voice of tranquil music.

But, alas! This kind heart had but a short time to remain such. The fatal poison of irresponsible power was already in her hands, and soon commenced its infernal work. That cheerful eye, under the influence of slavery, soon became red with rage; that voice, made all of sweet accord, changed to one of harsh and horrid discord; and that angelic face gave place to that of a demon.

Very soon after I went to live with Mr. and Mrs. Auld, she very kindly commenced to teach me the A, B, C. After I had learned this, she assisted me in learning to spell words of three or four letters. Just at this point of my progress, Mr. Auld found out what was going on, and at once forbade Mrs. Auld to instruct me further, telling her, among other things, that it was unlawful, as well as unsafe, to teach a slave to read. To use his own words, further, he said, "If you give a nigger an inch, he will take an ell. A nigger should know nothing but to obey his master—to do as he is told to do. Learning would *spoil* the best nigger in the world. Now," said he, "if you teach that nigger (speaking of myself) how to read, there would be no keeping him. It would forever unfit him to be a slave. He would at once become unmanageable, and of no value to his master. As to himself, it could do him no good, but a great deal of harm. It would make him discontented and unhappy." These words sank deep into my heart, stirred up sentiments within that lay slumbering, and called into existence an entirely new train of thought. It was a new and special revelation, explaining dark and mysterious things, with which my youthful understanding had struggled, but struggled in vain. I now understood what had been to me a most perplexing difficulty—to wit, the white man's power to enslave the black man. It was a grand achievement, and I prized it highly. From that moment, I understood the pathway from slavery to freedom. It was just what I wanted, and I got it at a time when I the least expected it. Whilst I was saddened by the thought of losing the aid of my kind mistress, I was gladdened by the invaluable instruction which, by the merest accident, I had gained from my master. Though conscious of the difficulty of learning without a teacher, I set out with high hope, and a fixed purpose, at whatever cost of trouble, to learn how to read. The very decided manner with which he spoke, and strove to impress his wife with the evil consequences of giving me instruction, served to convince me that he was deeply sensible of the truths he was uttering. It gave me the best assurance that I might rely with the utmost confidence on the results which, he said, would flow from teaching me to read. What he most dreaded, that I most desired. What he most loved, that I most hated. That which to him was a great evil, to be carefully shunned, was to me a great good, to be diligently sought; and the argument which he so warmly urged, against my learning to read, only served to inspire me with a desire and determination to learn. In learning to read, I owe almost as much to the bitter opposition of my master, as to the kindly aid of my mistress. I acknowledge the benefit of both. . . .

From Chapter 7

I lived in Master Hugh's family about seven years. During this time, I succeeded in learning to read and write. In accomplishing this, I was compelled to resort to various stratagems. I had no regular teacher. My mistress, who had kindly commenced to instruct me, had, in compliance with the advice and direction of her husband, not only ceased to instruct, but had set her face against my being instructed by anyone else. It is due, however, to my mistress to say of her, that she did not adopt this course of treatment immediately. She at first lacked the depravity indispensable to shutting me up in mental darkness. It was at least necessary for her to have some training in the exercise of irresponsible power, to make her equal to the task of treating me as though I were a brute.

My mistress was, as I have said, a kind and tenderhearted woman; and in the simplicity of her soul she commenced, when I first went to live with her, to treat me as she supposed one human being ought to treat another. In entering upon the duties of a slaveholder, she did not seem to perceive that I sustained to her the relation of a mere chattel, and that for her to treat me as a human being was not only wrong, but dangerously so. Slavery proved as injurious to her as it did to me. When I went there, she was a pious, warm, and tender-hearted woman. There was no sorrow or suffering for which she had not a tear. She had bread for the hungry, clothes for the naked, and comfort for every mourner that came within her reach. Slavery soon proved its ability to divest her of these heavenly qualities. Under its influence, the tender heart became stone, and the lamblike disposition gave way to one of tiger-like fierceness. The first step in her downward course was in her ceasing to instruct me. She now commenced to practice her husband's precepts. She finally became even more violent in her opposition than her husband himself. She was not satisfied with simply doing as well as he had commanded; she seemed anxious to do better. Nothing seemed to make her more angry than to see me with a newspaper. She seemed to think that here lay the danger. I have had her rush at me with a face made all up of fury, and snatch from me a newspaper, in a manner that fully revealed her apprehension. She was an apt woman; and a little experience soon demonstrated, to her satisfaction, that education and slavery were incompatible with each other.

From this time I was most narrowly watched. If I was in a separate room any considerable length of time, I was sure to be suspected of having a book, and was at once called to give an account of myself. All this, however, was too late. The first step had been taken. Mistress, in teaching me the alphabet, had given me the *inch*, and no precaution could prevent me from taking the *ell*.

The plan which I adopted, and the one by which I was most successful, was that of making friends of all the little white boys whom I met in the street. As many of these as I could, I converted into teachers. With their kindly aid, obtained at different times and in different places, I finally succeeded in learning to read. When I was sent of errands, I always took my book with me, and by going one part of my errand quickly, I found time to get a lesson before my return. I used also to carry bread with me, enough of which was always in the house, and to which I was always welcome; for I was much better off in this regard than many of the poor white children in our neighborhood. This bread I used to bestow upon the hungry little urchins, who, in return, would give me that more valuable bread of knowledge. I am strongly tempted to give the names of two or three of those little boys, as a testimonial of the gratitude and affection I bear them; but prudence forbids;—not that it would injure me, but it might embarrass them; for it is almost an unpardonable offence to teach slaves to read in this Christian country. . . .[1]

1. Describe what sort of people you believe Mr. and Mrs. Auld to be. List words or phrases that might describe their personalities and/or physical features.

2. Why do you think that the ability to read would make someone "forever unfit . . . to be a slave"? Have you ever read something that made you "discontented and unhappy," as Mr. Auld explained that Frederick would become? Describe your experience.

3. Draw the "pathway from slavery to freedom" that Douglass talks about. Label what events or ideas might appear on his pathway.

[1]Frederick Douglass, *Narrative of the Life of Frederick Douglass, An American Slave* (1845; reprint, New York: Dell Publishing, 1997), 32–34, 36–39.

Name _____

Date _____

Forging a Path

Directions: Describe an instance of metaphorical slavery, and the "pathway from slavery to freedom" that could be metaphorically traveled. Organize your ideas into a well-written composition.

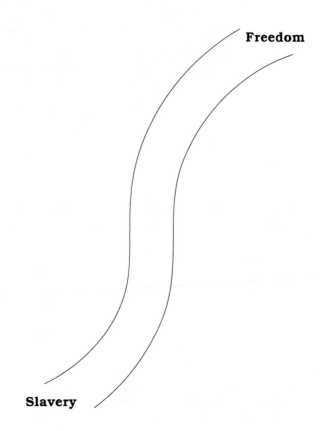

Calling Character into Question

Part A.

Directions: Refer to the passage in Frederick Douglass's narrative in which he describes Mrs. Auld's actions toward him. How did she change? Why did she change? Describe Mrs. Auld and her actions before her husband instructed her to stop teaching Douglass, and her actions after she stopped teaching him.

Before	After

Part B.

Directions: What do you believe is the most important message Douglass wants us to understand from his description of how "slavery proved as injurious to [Mrs. Auld] as it did to me"? Relate Douglass's ideas to society today. Explain your answer in a well-written paragraph.

Lesson 2
Quotable Quotes

Objectives
- To build a background for the themes of the novel
- To exercise critical thinking skills

Notes to the Teacher

James McBride's powerful memoir speaks to readers on several different levels. By means of different themes, we are taken along on his journey of self-discovery.

Lesson 2 prepares students to reflect on the themes of McBride's book by having them keep a journal. In this journal, students will respond to quotations that address the themes McBride presents in *The Color of Water*.

Paraphrasing—the ability to put others' ideas into our own words—is undoubtedly one of the most difficult skills to teach. Paraphrasing, and its companion, summarizing, are, however, learnable. Paraphrasing, moreover, is a skill that students will use after leaving school.

This journal is intended for forty daily practices in paraphrasing throughout the course of the book. You may wish to instruct students to keep **Handout 5**, a list of themes and quotations, in their journals and to refer to it for daily writing assignments at your direction. Or, you may prefer to write the daily quotation on an overhead projector or chalkboard. Note that the thematic sections may be used in any order. In fact, it is advisable to skip around in the handout when a quotation is especially pertinent to the assigned reading from *The Color of Water*. Many of the quotations make excellent starters for small or large group discussions.

The skill of paraphrasing has extra value in that it demands critical thinking by students. By putting ideas into their own words, and by detailing a practical application of the meaning of a quotation, students begin to develop this essential skill.

Procedure

1. On an overhead projector or chalkboard, write this quotation by Henry Ford: "You can't build a reputation on what you're going to do."

   Ask students to take notes to reinforce their comprehension of the following simple steps for paraphrasing quotations:

   a. Read the quotation carefully, using a dictionary to define any unfamiliar words

   b. Identify the key words and/or phrases in the quotation

   c. Put those key words and/or phrases into your own words, paraphrasing the other words as needed (This version should be as long as, or longer than, the original.)

   d. State how the quotation is relevant to you, to *The Color of Water*, to history, to the future, or to the world in general.

2. Take students through the four steps as you paraphrase Ford's quote.

   Suggested Responses:

   a. reputation—*known for having a specific quality or characteristic*

   b. *The key phrases seem to be "can't build a reputation" and "what you're going to do."*

   c. *People can't become respected based on plans they have made but have not yet accomplished.*

   d. *Perhaps the whole point of Ford's observation is that ideas without action are useless. Even the best idea will require hard work to make it successful.*

3. Distribute **Handout 4**. After reading Anna Pavlova's comment aloud, ask students to analyze what theme she might be discussing. *(Students may suggest that she is stating that success is achieved through hard work.)* Ask students to predict how this theme might apply to *The Color of Water*.

4. Using an overhead projector or chalkboard, walk students through this first journal exercise, asking for their assistance in modeling responses to the questions. Instruct students to keep this handout, because they will need to use its format for each daily entry into their journal. Establish a method for periodically collecting and grading these daily journal assignments.

5. Invite students to create posters that illustrate in some way the quotation, their paraphrase, and their application of the quotation. Make a colorful display in the classroom with these posters to reinforce the value expressed by the quotation.

6. Enhance students' oral presentation skills by assigning certain quotations to students to defend or to refute. First, allow students enough time to address the assigned quotation individually. Then, in pairs or small groups, have students select the paraphrase and application that best represents their opinions. Give them time (either in or out of class) to prepare either a defense or a refutation of the selected passage, expanding on their original application. Have pairs or groups present their ideas to each other.

7. Conduct the following whole class activity that emphasizes the importance of paraphrasing in speech: allow students time to respond individually to an assigned quotation, then go around the classroom and ask each student to contribute something different from what the previous student said. Although time-consuming, this exercise serves as a good closure activity that can work as a class opener the next day if it is not finished.

8. Students should read chapters 1–4 in preparation for Lesson 3. Before reading each chapter, students should write a prediction based on the chapter's title and record their predictions in a journal for later reflection.

Optional Activities

1. Paraphrase lyrics to a popular song. Then illustrate or present your paraphrases to small or large groups.

2. Research the importance that each individual quoted on **Handout 5** has had in history.

Name _____

Date _____

Quote, Unquote

Directions: Follow your teacher's instructions for this activity.

> As is the case in all branches of art, success depends in a very large measure upon individual initiative and exertion, and cannot be achieved except by dint of hard work.
>
> —Anna Pavlova

1. Define any unfamiliar words.

2. Identify the key words and/or phrases from the quotation.

3. Paraphrase the quotation.

4. Explain how this quotation is related to you, to history, to the future, or to the world in general.

Name _____

Date _____

May I Quote You?

Directions: Use the four-step paraphrasing process to address each assigned quotation.

Theme: Education

"To be conscious that you are ignorant is a great step to knowledge."
> —Benjamin Disraeli

"Education makes a people easy to lead, but difficult to drive; easy to govern, but impossible to enslave."
> —Lord Brougham

"The things taught in schools and colleges are not an education, but the means to an education."
> —Ralph Waldo Emerson

"Imagination is more important than knowledge."
> —Albert Einstein

"When I was a boy of fourteen, my father was so ignorant I could hardly stand to have the old man around. But when I got to be twenty-one, I was astonished at how much he had learned in seven years."
> —Mark Twain

Theme: Dreams and Goals

"When we can't dream any longer, we die."
> —Emma Goldman

"If you have built castles in the air, your work need not be lost; that is where they should be; now put foundations under them."
> —Henry David Thoreau

"To be what we are, and to become what we are capable of becoming, is the only end to life."
> —Robert Louis Stevenson

"I was not looking for my dreams to interpret my life, but rather for my life to interpret my dreams."
> —Susan Sontag

Theme: Journeys and Growth

"Start where you are, with what you have. Make something of it. Never be satisfied."
> —George Washington Carver

"It is never too late to be what you might have been."
> —George Eliot

"You must do the thing you think you cannot do."
> —Eleanor Roosevelt

"One doesn't discover new lands without consenting to lose sight of the shore for a very long time."
> —André Gide

"Never look back unless you are planning to go that way."
> —Anonymous

Theme: Helping Others

"The good we secure for ourselves is precarious and uncertain . . . until it is secured for all of us, and incorporated into our common life."

—Jane Addams

"Some day, after we have mastered the winds, the waves, the tides, and gravity, we shall harness for God the energies of love; then, for the second time in the history of the world, man will have discovered fire."

—Pierre Teilhard de Chardin

"The worst sin toward our fellow creatures is not to hate them, but to be indifferent to them: that's the essence of inhumanity."

—George Bernard Shaw

"When we grow old, there can only be one regret—not to have given enough of ourselves."

—Eleanora Duse

Theme: Preparing for the Future

"Our children may learn about heroes of the past. Our task is to make ourselves architects of the future."

—Jomo Mzee Kenyatta

"We cannot always build the future for our youth, but we can build our youth for the future."

—Franklin D. Roosevelt

"We only want that which is given naturally to all peoples of the world, to be masters of our own fate, not of others', and in cooperation and friendship with others."

—Golda Meir

Theme: Erasing Prejudice

"One's life has value so long as one attributes value to the life of others, by means of love, friendship, indignation, and compassion."

—Simone de Beauvoir

"Make no judgments where you have no compassion."

—Anne McCaffrey

"[Bigotry's] birthplace is the sinister back room of the mind where plots and schemes are hatched for the persecution and oppression of other human beings."

—Bayard Rustin

Theme: Courage

"Courage is resistance to fear, mastery of fear—not absence of fear."

—Mark Twain

"It is a brave act of valor to condemn death; but where life is more terrible than death, it is then the truest valor to dare to live."

—François de La Rochefoucauld

"None but a coward dares to boast that he has never known fear."

—Marshal Ferdinand Foch

Theme: Facing Challenges

"Challenges make you discover things about yourself that you never really knew. They're what make the instrument stretch—what make you go beyond the norm."

—Cicely Tyson

"If you have made mistakes . . . there is always another chance for you . . . you may have a fresh start any moment you choose, for this thing we call 'failure' is not the falling down, but the staying down."

—Mary Pickford

"There are no problems, only decisions."

—Robert W. Schuller

"Stumbling is not falling."

—Portuguese proverb

Theme: Important Choices

"Once again she decided not to decide. She preferred being compelled into her decisions."

—Lisa Alther

"A peacefulness follows any decision, even the wrong one."

—Rita Mae Brown

"We know what happens to people who stay in the middle of the road. They get run over."

—Aneurin Bevan

"We choose our joys and sorrows long before we experience them."

—Kahlil Gibran

"Fate chooses our relatives; we choose our friends."

—Jacques Delille

Theme: The Rewards of Work

"The harder you work, the luckier you get."

—Gary Player

"Far and away the best prize that life offers is the chance to work hard at work worth doing."
—Theodore Roosevelt

" . . . there is as much dignity in tilling a field as in writing a poem."
—Booker T. Washington

"Work is not a curse; it is the prerogative of intelligence, the only means to manhood, and the measure of civilization. Savages do not work."

—Calvin Coolidge

Lesson 3
A Family Affair

Objectives
- To understand the development of characters
- To note the use of voice

Notes to the Teacher

James McBride's family could be described by today's pop psychologists as "dysfunctional." Any one of several daytime television talk shows would love to have him or his siblings as guests! Yet every one of his brothers and sisters felt loved and valued, felt that he or she held an important and special place in the family's order.

Lesson 3 presents students with a close look at McBride's family, how it functioned, and aspects of its characterization. Students should be encouraged to draw parallels between their own families and McBride's.

Procedure

1. Ask students to review their predictions for each chapter (see procedure 8, Lesson 2). Were they accurate? How did their predictions differ from actual content? Students may share their ideas with a partner.

2. Review the literary concept of *voice* with students. Voice is a sense of presence, intelligence, and moral sensibility shown by a literary character. Inform students that voice determines how much information we receive about a character, both in fiction and nonfiction.

3. Identify the voices used in chapters 1–4. (*chapter 1—Ruth; chapter 2—McBride; chapter 3—Ruth; chapter 4—McBride*) Ask students to hypothesize why McBride chose this voice pattern, which he uses for much of the book. (*Students may suggest that McBride can comment on his mother's observations or add his own to hers through use of this pattern.*)

4. Ask students to describe Ruth's family life from chapter 1 and share their descriptions with a partner. Invite students to recount some of Ruth's experiences.

5. Ruth's terse account of her background is intense. Highlight the enigma of her remark that "Rachel Shilsky is dead as far as I'm concerned. She had to die in order for me, the rest of me, to live." Discuss this concept. Instruct students to write a composition in which they describe how they or someone they know has had to give up something—die, in a sense—so that they could "live." Specify your criteria for a well-written composition before students begin this assignment.

6. Shift students' focus to the development of characterization. Remind students that authors reveal their characters to us in three basic ways—through direct description; through the characters' own actions, speech, or thoughts; or through the responses of other characters.

7. Chapter 2 contains brief characterizations of the author's stepfather, Hunter Jordan, and his mother. Reread the second paragraph of chapter 2 aloud. Ask students to determine what aspects of his stepfather's character McBride is describing (*physical attributes, personality, love of family*).

8. Engage students in these characterizations by distributing **Handout 6**. Focus their attention on part A. Discuss students' answers for part A before assigning part B as homework.

9. Continue the discussion of characterization by asking students to list some of Ruth's character traits as described in chapter 2. (*She is completely unaware of what others think of her; she maintains a nonchalance about the dangers she faces as a white woman in an all-black neighborhood; she does not socialize with others; she has odd or strange habits; and she gets her children into college through the sheer force of her willpower.*)

10. In a manner true to her nature, Ruth gave advice to McBride when he was just a kindergartner asking her questions about why she didn't look like the other mothers: "You ask too many questions. Educate your mind. School is important. Forget Rodney and Pete. Forget their mothers. You remember school. Forget everything else. Who cares about Rodney and Pete! When they go one way, you go the other way. Understand? When they go one way, you go the other way. You hear me?"

Ask students to respond to her brusque manner. What do they think it conceals? (*Students may suggest that beneath her brusque manner lies someone who knows how tough life will be for her children; perhaps she's trying to prepare them as children for what lies ahead.*)

11. Distribute **Handout 7**. As a means of fostering understanding prior to this exercise, remind students that McBride says "it was killed or be killed in my house, and Mommy . . . created the system. You were left to your own devices or so you thought until you were at your very wits' end, at which time she would step in and rescue you." Invite students to imagine how they would fare in such a household.

    This assignment may be expanded into a full-length comparison/contrast composition at your discretion.

12. In chapter 3, Ruth relates the journey her ancestors made in coming to America. Distribute **Handout 8**. This is to be a long-term project, due at the conclusion of *The Color of Water*. Discuss how this assignment can be completed.

13. Refer students to quotations from **Handout 5** (Lesson 2) that would be appropriate to address in this lesson.

14. Review with students the definition of allusion they learned in Lesson 1. Instruct them to determine the allusion of the title of chapter 4, "Black Power." (*Black Power was an African-American movement of the 1960s inspired by Malcolm X and named by Stokely Carmichael. It questioned the goals of the civil rights movement; adhered to Malcolm X's beliefs in separatism, black ownership of factories and businesses, and vigorous defense against white aggression; supporters opposed integration into white society.*)

15. Distribute **Handout 9**. In pairs, students should discuss each of the Black Panthers' points with their own opinions; then they should address each point as Ruth would. Direct students' attention to the thirtieth paragraph in chapter 4, where

McBride describes the extent of the influence of Black Power in his neighborhood. Have students reread this section through to the end of the chapter.

Suggested Responses:

1. *Ruth might tell her children that their destiny would be determined by education and religion.*

2. *Ruth worked the swing shift as a typist, putting in eleven-hour days. She would have had no patience for anything less than "full employment."*

3. *Ruth knew firsthand how blacks were often taken advantage of, having seen her father do it many times.*

4. *Ruth's home was always chaotic. Any shelter would suffice.*

5. *Education was the key to all success, Ruth believed; therefore, she sent her children to white schools, believing they would get a better education there.*

6. *Ruth believed in fulfilling her duties. She probably would not have approved of someone's being exempt.*

7. *Ruth would agree, believing that "white folks . . . were implicitly evil toward blacks. . . ."*

9. *Students should support their opinions with examples from the text.*

10. *Ruth preferred to live among the poor, so she would have been familiar with their needs for these items.*

16. We are afforded another glimpse of Ruth's character in chapter 4, when McBride tells us her motto: "If it doesn't involve your going to school or church, I could care less about it and my answer is no whatever it is." Instruct students to do the following for homework: create their own mottos, or write ones for other people. Post their creations around the room.

17. Develop an understanding of Ruth by examining the apparent contradictions of her character that McBride describes in the last half of chapter 4. Lead students in a discussion of these contradictions.

18. Reinforce students' critical thinking skills with **Handout 10**. Students may work individually or in pairs on this assignment. Encourage students to respond on both literal and figurative levels.

Suggested Responses:

1. Kaddish is a prayer recited in daily synagogue services and by mourners after the death of a close relative. Shiva is a period of seven days of mourning after the death of a close relative.

2. When Ruth left her home, she left her family behind her. In effect, they shunned her because of her choices.

4. McBride failed his high school classes; he hung out with his friends, committing petty crimes and using drugs. He even robbed a drug dealer.

19. Assign chapters 5–8 in preparation for Lesson 4. In their journals, students should record a prediction based on each chapter's title.

Optional Activities

1. Research some of the rituals and tenets of Judaism that Ruth mentions, and then report your findings to the class.

2. Search the Internet for more information about the 1960s civil rights movement and the Black Panther Party. Present your findings to the class.

3. McBride alludes to many famous historical figures in chapter 4. Research their significance in the civil rights movement.

The Building Blocks of Character

Part A.

Directions: How does McBride characterize his stepfather? Fill out the chart below. Paraphrase or use direct quotations from the text.

Physical Attributes

Personality

Love of Family

Part B.

Directions: Using McBride's model, create a one-paragraph characterization of a person you know well.

Name _____

Date _____

Home Is Heaven for Beginners

Directions: Use chapters 1–4 as a basis for comparing and contrasting McBride's household with your own. Complete the chart.

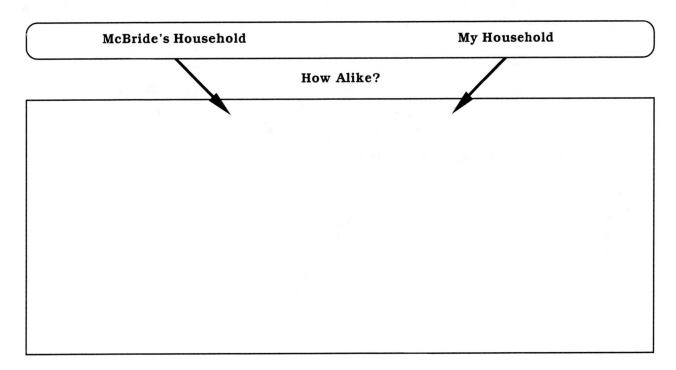

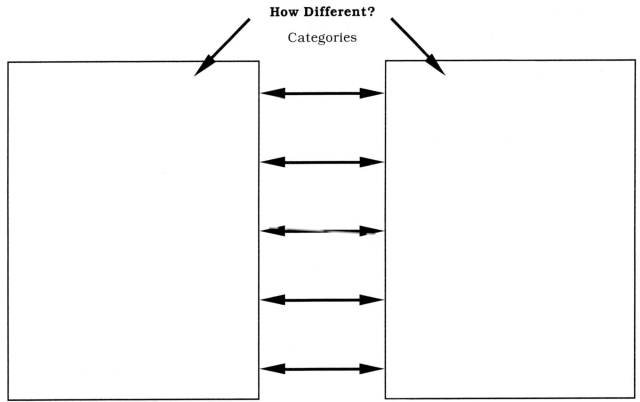

Name _____

Date _____

Coming to America

Directions: If information is available, trace your ancestors' journey to America, much as Ruth does in chapter 3. Enlist your family members in this endeavor to ensure that you are as complete and accurate as possible. If information is not available, trace the journey of the ancestors of a celebrity or of someone close to you. Present your results as a map.

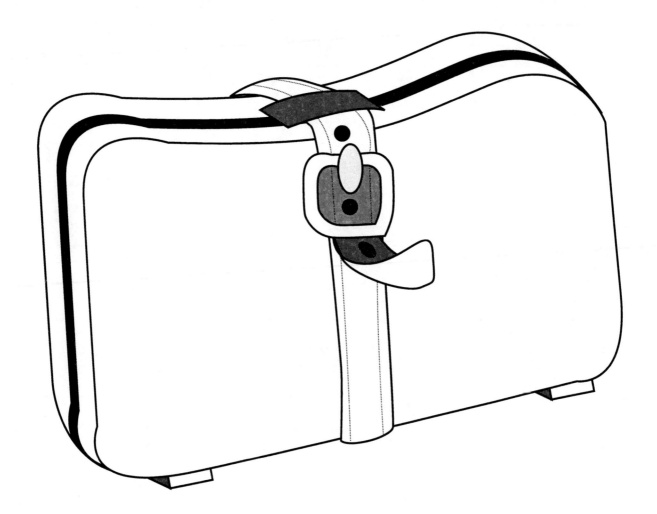

Name _____

Date _____

Black Power!

Directions: Refer to chapter 4 when comparing the Black Panthers' beliefs with those of Ruth McBride Jordan.

Black Panthers	Ruth McBride Jordan
1. WE WANT freedom. We want power to determine the destiny of our Black Community.	
2. WE WANT full employment for our people.	
3. WE WANT an end to the robbery by the capitalist community.	
4. WE WANT decent housing, fit for the shelter of human beings.	
5. WE WANT education for our people that exposes the true nature of this decadent American society.	
6. WE WANT all black men to be exempt from military service.	
7. WE WANT an immediate end to POLICE BRUTALITY and MURDER of black people.	
8. WE WANT freedom for all black men held in federal, state, county and city prisons and jails.	
9. WE WANT all black people when brought to trial to be tried in court by a jury of their peer group or people from their black communities, as defined by the Constitution of the United States.	
10. WE WANT land, bread, housing, education, clothing, justice, and peace.	

¹Excerpted from the Black Panther Party Platform and Program, October 1996. Available online at http://www.cs.oberlin.edu/students/pjaques/etext/bpp-program.html; Accessed 9 September 1999.

Name _____

Date _____

Reading between the Lines

Directions: After reading chapters 1–4, answer the following questions.

1. Using context clues, define *kaddish* and *shiva*.

2. Explain why Ruth's family considered her to be dead.

3. Explain what you think Ruth could have meant by the last line of chapter 1.

4. Delineate how the death of McBride's stepfather affected McBride.

5. List five descriptive adjectives for Ruth's tone in chapter 3.

Lesson 4
Faith—The Foundation

Objectives

- To analyze the importance of faith in the characters' lives

- To reinforce the values of determination and perseverance

Notes to the Teacher

Without a doubt, a spiritual foundation is important in the life of Ruth McBride Jordan. In her opinion, without education and church, people's lives meant nothing. Without proselytizing, McBride offers a perspective of the workings of faith in the author's life.

Chapters 5–8 present opportunities for readers to examine Ruth's faith and how it colored all she did. Students should be encouraged to view Ruth's faith and beliefs with an open mind. They do not have to agree or disagree; they are studying them to learn from them. Students will continue to explore the element of characterization.

Note that chapter 5 reveals the sexual abuse that Ruth endured as a child. Some students may be particularly sensitive to this issue.

Procedure

1. Use a Venn diagram (interlocking circles) for students to record similarities and differences between their predictions for chapters 5–8 and the events that McBride relates. Allow students to share these aloud.

2. Focus students' attention on the lesson by asking them to think about where they live now. Ask them:

   - Have you always lived where you live now?

   - If not, where did you live before, and how long ago did you move?

   - Why did you move?

   - What were the most difficult aspects of moving from one place to another?

3. Ask paired students to list the effects on children of moving every year or so, as Ruth's family did. Request that pairs share their observations with the class.

4. Invite students to examine part A of **Handout 11**. Allow them about ten minutes to complete the organizer. Then, as they brainstorm, students may wish to refer to the end of chapter 8 and the difficulties that McBride's sister Helen encounters. Ask students to share their ideas with others.

   Assign part B to be completed outside of class. Specify the criteria for a well-written composition before students begin writing.

5. Psychologists today believe that family abuse goes in cycles—parents abuse their children; their children grow up to abuse their own children; those children, too, become abusers. Certainly, Ruth's upbringing would meet the definition of abuse. So why did she not abuse her children in turn? Discuss possible reasons with the class; then distribute **Handout 12**. Students may complete this individually or in small groups. Students may use this study of characterization as the basis for a character analysis.

6. Remind students to refer to the quotations from **Handout 5** (Lesson 2) as they continue keeping their journals.

7. As narrated in chapters 5 and 8, Ruth's family moved to Virginia in 1929. Assign student pairs to research racial conditions in the South at that time. Students should prepare a visual aid for display that presents the information they have discovered.

8. Discuss symbolism as a literary device. Symbolism is the use of one idea or thing to represent something else.

   For example, a writer wishing to show the incredible size of a task or a job may compare it by saying, "The task loomed before me, as menacing as Mount Everest." Ask students what may be symbolic about the title of Chapter 5, "The Old Testament." (*Students may point out that in the popular mind, the Old Testament sometimes seems like history, much as Ruth considers her own history to be "put away."*)

9. Enhance students' appreciation of McBride's description of church services in chapter 6 by obtaining a recording of African-American gospel music such as that by Kirk Franklin or by showing a brief film clip from a movie such as *The Preacher's Wife*, starring Whitney Houston and Denzel Washington, or *The Apostle*, starring Robert Duvall. Students whose church experiences differ from these charismatic and energetic examples will find a new appreciation for McBride's experiences.

10. Continue the lesson by rereading the section of chapter 6 where young James asks his mother about the color of God. Assign **Handout 13** for homework. Stress that for this activity, student responses will be kept entirely confidential because of their introspective nature. Allow students to keep this piece and to refine it as they read the book.

11. To lend closure to this lesson, distribute **Handout 14**. Before assigning part B, make students aware of the various formats for writing letters. Most grammar and composition books have models.

12. Direct students to read chapters 9–12 in preparation for Lesson 5. Remind them to record a prediction based on each chapter's title in their journals.

Optional Activity

Prepare part B of **Handout 14** as a speech, and deliver it to the class.

Name _____

Date _____

One of a Dozen

Part A.

Directions: Use the organizer to consider the challenges you would have to face if you were part of a family of twelve children as McBride was.

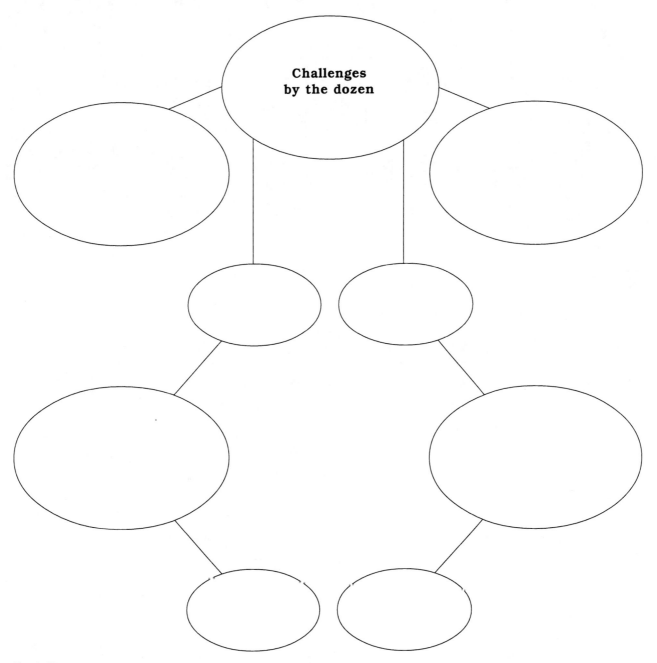

Part B.

Directions: In a well-written composition, discuss how you would meet each of the challenges of being part of a large family.

Name _____

Date _____

The Strength to Overcome

Directions: Examine the strengths of character that allow Ruth to defeat a cycle of abuse.

Strength 1

_____

Supporting details:

Strength 2

_____

Supporting details:

Ruth's
Strengths
of
Character

Strength 3

_____

Supporting detaills:

Strength 4

_____

Supporting details:

Name _____

Date _____

The Color of God

Directions: Examine your own feelings about God. How does spirituality manifest itself in your own life? What color do you believe God is? How would you explain this to a child?

Name _____

Date _____

It's Apparent

Part A.

Directions: Compare and contrast Ruth's abilities as a parent with the abilities of one or both of your own parents or guardians, using chapters 5–8 as your reference. Record both similarities and differences here.

Ruth   **My Parent(s)/Guardian(s)**

Differences   *Similarities*   *Differences*

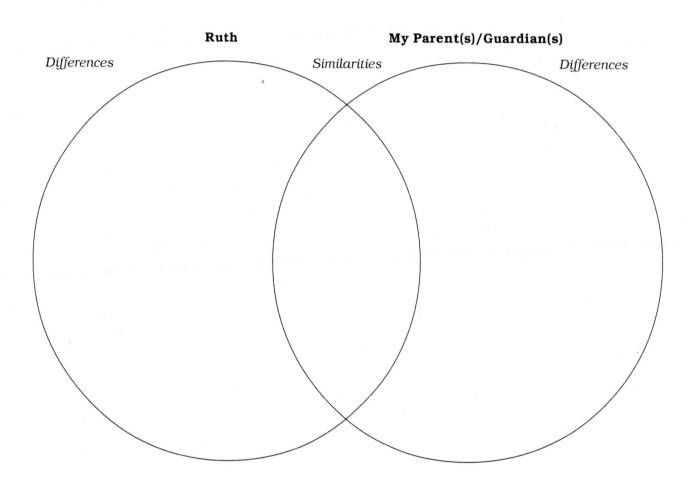

Part B.

Directions: Imagine you have been asked to nominate either Ruth or your own parent(s)/guardian(s) as "Parent of the Year." Compose a letter to the judging committee. Consider using "A Tribute to _____" as a title.

Lesson 5
A Historical Legacy

Objectives

- To research the historical background of *The Color of Water*

- To focus on the development of characterization

Notes to the Teacher

James McBride's large family, his Jewish mother and African-American father, his poverty, and his ancestral history all shaped his own life. His family would certainly symbolize the belief of Abram Joseph Ryan, a Confederate Army chaplain, who wrote that "a land without ruins is a land without memories—a land without memories is a land without history." As Jews and African Americans, McBride's family had a historical legacy that affected them long after the first slaves were brought to this country.

It will be necessary to set aside class time for student research or to assign out-of-class research. Various Internet resources for research are included in the lesson plans. Lesson 5 will continue to draw on information presented in previous chapters and objectives addressed in previous lessons.

Procedure

1. Have pairs of students share their predictions for each chapter as they did for Lesson 2, procedure 10. Students should note accurate predictions and any differences between their predictions and the events of the narrative.

2. Chapter 9 presents a poignant picture of one of Ruth's few pleasant childhood memories. Students will relate to her delight in her friendship with Frances. Solicit examples of childhood friendships from the class to set the tone for **Handout 15**. Students may retain this piece in a portfolio for further review and refinement.

3. Engage students in the lesson by asking them to visualize the American South before the civil rights movement of the 1960s. On an overhead projector or chalkboard, record the images students share. (*Students*

may note the prejudice and violence directed toward African Americans, but point out that Southern racists were "equal opportunity" offenders—they also targeted Jews, Catholics, and immigrants.)

4. Point out to students that although African Americans and Jews have much in common—a shared experience of being the objects of hate and prejudice—they have often been at odds with each other. Ruth discusses this dichotomy in chapter 10. Students may also note that the Reverend Louis Farrakhan, an African American, more recently has been accused of anti-Semitism. Ask students to examine why the two minorities sometimes conflict.

5. Write the following five lines from Langston Hughes's poem "Theme for English B" on a chalkboard or overhead projector:

   The instructor said,
   > *Go home and write*
   > *a page tonight.*
   > *And let that page come out of you—*
   > *Then, it will be true.*

6. Have students comment about how they might interpret such an assignment. What does the instructor expect? What does the instructor hope students will do? What would they include in such an assignment? Students may write their responses in a journal.

7. Refer students to **Handout 16**. Solicit a student volunteer to read Hughes's powerful poem aloud. Then place students in groups to complete part A of the activity.

Suggested Responses:

2. *The instructor directed students to "go home," and Hughes described the exact route he took to do so. Asked to "write a page," Hughes did precisely that. As for the writing being "true," Hughes wrote about his own experiences, thereby insuring the honesty of his writing.*

3. *Students may note that the long distance he is required to walk each day to college suggests a dedication to school; they may also point out that his neighborhood seems a less favorable one than his instructor's.*

4. *Perhaps "on the hill above Harlem" symbolizes the exalted status that education has in Hughes's mind.*

5. *Line 11 refers to Hughes's steps as "lead[ing] down into Harlem," a more negative image than the exalted college "on the hill."*

7. *Hughes is African American, while his instructor is white; Hughes is younger than his instructor; the instructor is "somewhat more free" than Hughes.*

8. Assign part B of **Handout 16**. Give students an extended period of time in which to complete this prose-poem, perhaps polishing it for their portfolios. Invite students to share their poems aloud when completed.

9. Lead a discussion about characterization. Invite students to recall a time in their own lives when they felt like an outsider, someone different from everyone else. Students may record these recollections in their journals.

10. Students will sympathize with McBride's own experiences as an outcast, usually the only African-American student in his classes. Draw on this emotion in reviewing with the class McBride's search for identity in chapter 10. He even became ashamed of Ruth. Check that students understand McBride's appreciation as an adult for the privilege of having a mixed heritage, even though as a child he sought to escape it.

11. Refer students to quotations from **Handout 5** (Lesson 2) that would be appropriate to address in this lesson and write about in their journals.

12. To facilitate students' understanding, ask them to review the portion of chapter 10 where McBride retreats into an imaginary world. Pose the following questions for class discussion:

    • Who is the boy in the mirror that McBride describes?

    • What did McBride hate about him? Why?

Student answers will vary but must be supported with examples from text.

13. Examine **Handout 17** with students. This is a highly introspective piece, and students may have difficulty. Encourage students to be as honest as possible. Specify your criteria for a well-written composition before students begin to write.

14. Perhaps the most poignant chapter in *The Color of Water*, chapter 11 describes the dreams Ruth has. Those dreams lead her into an unplanned teenage pregnancy; the father of her child, another teenager. To compound trouble, Peter, the young man Ruth loves, is African American.

15. Process with students the types of difficulties that young Ruth and Peter would encounter in their situation. (*Students may comment that the two teens must overcome racial prejudice, possible physical violence directed at Peter, fear of the unknown, fear over the pregnancy.*)

16. Distribute **Handout 18** to students. Develop a definition of a narrative (*an expository piece that tells a story*). Encourage students to be as in-character as possible, perhaps even emulating Ruth's voice.

17. Chapters 10–12 provide a fascinating glimpse into the history that Ruth McBride Jordan and Hunter Jordan, Sr. lived. Direct students to research an aspect of the characters' lives as presented in the book. Pair or group students to assist each other in their research.

Provide the following research topics and related Web sites:

• typical life for African Americans in 1940s and '50s in the South

• Jim Crow laws (http://www.nps.gov/malu/documents/ jim crow laws.htm)

• anti-Semitism in the United States

• New York, the Roaring Twenties and the Prohibition movement

(http://www.druglibrary.org/schaffer/ LIBRARY/studies/nc/nc2a.htm)

Specify the length and type of research product you desire before students begin the assignment. Students should be prepared to present their research findings orally to their classmates.

18. McBride eloquently describes his relationship with the man he knew as "Daddy," Hunter Jordan, Sr. Students will relate to McBride's shyness in chapter 12 when he wishes to tell Daddy how much he loves him. Instruct students to write about a time when they may have wanted to say something important but could not. Ask them to describe the initial situation and the end results. Because of the personal nature of this activity, students may wish to refine this piece only for their portfolios.

19. Direct students to read chapters 13–16 in preparation for Lesson 6. Students should record a prediction based on each chapter's title in their journals.

Optional Activities

1. Read more of Langston Hughes's work—particularly *Montage of a Dream Deferred*, from which "Theme for English B" is taken.

2. Visit http://www.redhotjazz.com/hughes.html on the Internet for more information on Hughes.

Name _____

Date _____

The Bird, a Nest; the Spider, a Web; Man, Friendship

Directions: Poet William Blake believed friends are as necessary to humans as homes are to other creatures. Describe a childhood friendship with someone you'll never forget, a friendship like Ruth's with Frances. Complete the following organizer.

When We Met	How We Met

Our Activities

Similarities	Differences

The Value of This Friendship

"Theme for English B"

Part A.

Directions: Read the poem, and answer the questions.

The instructor said,

> *Go home and write*
> *a page tonight.*
> *And let that page come out of you—*   5
> *Then, it will be true.*

I wonder if it's that simple?

I am twenty-two, colored, born in Winston-Salem.
I went to school there, then Durham, then here
to this college on the hill above Harlem.
I am the only colored student in my class.   10
The steps from the hill lead down into Harlem,
through a park, then I cross St. Nicholas,
Eighth Avenue, Seventh, and I come to the Y,
the Harlem Branch Y, where I take the elevator
up to my room, sit down, and write this page: 15

It's not easy to know what is true for you or me
at twenty-two, my age. But I guess I'm what
I feel and see and hear, Harlem, I hear you:
hear you, hear me—we two—you, me, talk on this page.
(I hear New York, too.) Me—who?   20

Well, I like to eat, sleep, drink, and be in love.
I like to work, read, learn, and understand life.
I like a pipe for a Christmas present,
or records—Bessie, bop, or Bach.
I guess being colored doesn't make me *not* like   25
the same things other folks like who are other races.

So will my page be colored that I write?
Being me, it will not be white.
But it will be
a part of you, instructor.   30
You are white—
yet a part of me, as I am a part of you.
That's American.
Sometimes perhaps you don't want to be a part of me.
Nor do I often want to be a part of you.   35
But we are, that's true!
As I learn from you,
I guess you learn from me—
although you're older—and white—
and somewhat more free.   40
This is my page for English B.[1]

---

[1]Langston Hughes, "Theme for English B," *Montage of a Dream Deferred* (New York: Henry Holt, 1951), 39–40.

1. This poem was written in 1951. List what you know about what life was like for African Americans at that time.

2. Describe how Langston Hughes's poem follows his instructor's directions exactly.

3. What does Hughes's route suggest about him?

4. Refer to line 9 of the poem. What does the phrase "on the hill above Harlem" suggest?

5. How do the images in line 11 differ from the image in line 9?

6. Study lines 34 and 35. Do you think Hughes's statement here is an honest discussion of his and perhaps our society? Explain your response.

7. Explain how Hughes and his instructor are similar and different.

Part B.

Directions: Write your own "Theme for English." Begin your composition with the first five lines of Hughes' poem, adding another thirty to thirty-five lines as he did.

The Color of Water
Lesson 5
Handout 17

Through the Looking-Glass

Directions: Describe the person in your mirror. Do you like whom you see? Explain how you are similar to or different from James McBride's "boy in the mirror." Present your thoughts in a well-written composition.

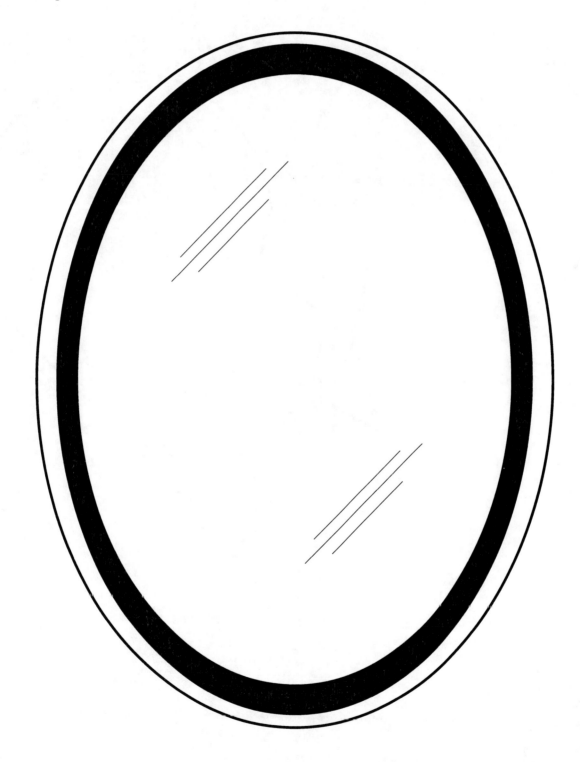

Name _____

Date _____

Forbidden Fruit

Directions: Take on the persona of either Ruth or Peter. Write a narrative of what you're feeling, thinking, and planning as you realize you're in love with someone whom society forbids you to love.

Lesson 6
A Journey of Self-Discovery

Objectives

- To examine the value of education

- To evaluate McBride's journey of self-discovery

- To read and react to the narrated events

Notes to the Teacher

Most of us can recall a time when we thought of running away, of removing ourselves from a troublesome situation. James McBride and his mother are no different. Students will identify with the dilemmas that these two face in chapters 13–16 as they encounter seemingly insurmountable problems.

In Lesson 6, students will study how the author and his mother faced difficult dilemmas. Through their struggles, both managed to advance on their journeys of self-discovery; indeed, they discover that they are stronger people than they had ever imagined.

Procedure

1. Ask students to revisit their predictions for chapters 13–16. Have them note similarities and differences between those predictions and the actual events of the story.

2. On an overhead projector or chalkboard, brainstorm with students the reasons that people have for running away or for trying to escape their problems. Conduct a brief discussion of these ideas. Suggest that, as Albert Einstein said, "In the middle of difficulty lies opportunity." Solicit student input on Einstein's words.

3. Review the meaning of *metaphor*, a comparison of two unlike things without the use of *like* or *as*. Ask students: Metaphorically speaking, what are some ways that people can run away? (*Students might note that running away can metaphorically happen by withdrawing from friends and family, using drugs or alcohol, burying oneself in work or school, or denying or ignoring problems altogether.*)

4. Continue this discussion of running away with **Handout 19**. The purpose of this survey is to gather opinions about escaping problems from both students' peer group and adults. To facilitate easy surveying, model for students how they might approach their peers and adults for answers to their questions.

5. Emphasize that because a good survey will question a variety of people, students should attempt to sample teens who are not all alike, and to sample adults of varying ages and occupations. Students may begin by asking these questions of other students in the classroom. The rest of the assignment should be done outside of class. The number of people surveyed is left to the teacher's discretion. Students should be prepared to discuss and/or present their findings to their classmates.

6. Use the quotations for critical thinking exercises in students' journals as they continue reading Lesson 6. Refer to Lesson 2, procedures 1–4.

7. Divide the class into four sections, one each for chapters 13–16. Within each section, place students into groups of three. Assign roles of recorder, timer, and checker to group members:

   - Timer will note the time limit given at your discretion and will monitor time.

   - Checker will ask group what points should be shared with the rest of the class.

   - Recorder will list these points on paper.

8. Distribute **Handout 20,** part A to student groups. Instruct groups that they are to locate the problems that McBride or his mother faces in the chapters assigned to them, list them in the appropriate place on the handout, and discuss how each person handled those difficulties. Group recorders should then write these points.

9. Have groups present their pieces of the jigsaw puzzle to the rest of the class. All students will record the new information on the handout.

10. Distribute **Handout 20,** part B. Students should review their responses from part A to assist them in responding to part B individually.

Suggested Responses:

Chapter 13—*Ruth was able to turn her unplanned pregnancy into an opportunity with the help of her mother, who sent her to New York and away from the difficulties at home.*

Chapter 14—*James didn't turn the difficulty of his stepfather's death into an opportunity.*

Chapter 15—*Ruth overcomes her hurt at Peter's betrayal and graduates from high school. She stays true to Judaism, even though she began to have her own opinions. She leaves Virginia for New York.*

Chapter 16—*Once again, James allows his personal difficulties to remain unsurmounted.*

11. Help students discover that in chapter 13, Ruth temporarily escapes her problems in Virginia but encounters new obstacles in New York. Ask students to list these new obstacles. (*She's in an unfamiliar city; she must depend on the kindness of family members who are almost strangers; she's dealing with her pregnancy and subsequent abortion; she's undoubtedly lonely for her mother and sister.*)

12. In addition to her own difficulties, Ruth must deal with those of her relatives. Discuss these problems. (*She mentions that they had work, children, and problems of their own. Furthermore, Ruth notes that her extended family were "all trying hard to be American . . . not knowing what to keep and what to leave behind."*)

13. Informally poll students, asking if any of them have experienced the dilemma of "trying hard to be American . . . not knowing what to keep and what to leave behind." Distribute **Handout 21** for students to complete individually in class or for homework. Discuss responses in the next class.

Suggested Responses:

1. *the American flag; hot dogs and apple pie; blonde dolls with blue eyes; football; Bill and Daisy (all-American names)*

2. *Perhaps Ruth's relatives wanted to be American because they thought that would be the surest route to success and the American Dream.*

3. *Immigrants may choose to Americanize their children so that they fit in with the new culture that their parents have chosen for them.*

14. Turn students' attention to James in chapters 14 and 16. Many students will know teenagers like James. Point out that he is a picture of how bad choices consume us. Running away from his grief over his stepfather's death and his loneliness, James turns to alcohol, drugs, crime, and bad company. He is almost killed, but he won't stop. He fails school. His efforts to hide from himself draws him closer to his friends and apart from his family.

15. Emphasize that James McBride as a teenager finds himself getting back at the world for his suffering, fighting against injustices he can't name. He feels beleaguered by his mother and the world in general. He stuffs his feelings of grief and loneliness and anger inside, and he uses marijuana and alcohol to forget his pain. Unfortunately, his pain and guilt increase, and his problems with drugs get worse proportionally.

16. Distribute **Handout 22**. Students may wish to compose their responses in prose or poetry. Allow them to retain this piece in their portfolios for further refinement. (Students may be allowed to write about someone other than themselves.)

17. Direct students' attention to the wonderful advice McBride's sister Jack gives him in chapter 16. Distribute **Handout 23** and permit students to polish this piece while they finish reading the novel.

18. Assign chapters 17–20 in preparation for Lesson 7. Remind students to record predictions in their journals.

Optional Activity

The author confides in chapter 16 that he is addicted to marijuana. Research the addictive properties of marijuana and other drugs, and present your findings to the class.

Name _____

Date _____

On the Run

Directions: Survey teens and adults with the following questions to determine their impressions about running away.

1. What causes people to want to run away?

2. What are some examples of people who have run away?

3. Would you advise someone to run away? Why or why not?

4. What problems may develop from running away?

5. What solutions are better than running away?

Name _____

Date _____

Difficulty or Opportunity?

Part A.

Directions: Refer to chapters 13–16 in *The Color of Water*. In each chapter, record the difficulties that McBride or his mother faces which might suggest the possibility of running away.

Chapter 13

Chapter 14

Chapter 15

Chapter 16

Part B.

Directions: How could Ruth McBride Jordan and James McBride have turned their difficulties into opportunities? When did they succeed in doing so?

Chapter 13

Chapter 14

Chapter 15

Chapter 16

Name _____

Date _____

Trying Hard to Be American

Directions: Read the poem, and answer the questions that follow it.

Immigrants

wrap their babies in the American flag,
feed them mashed hot dogs and apple pie,
name them Bill and Daisy,
buy them blonde dolls that blink blue
eyes or a football and tiny cleats
before the baby can even walk,
speak to them in thick English,
   hallo, babee, hallo
whisper in Spanish or Polish
when the babies sleep, whisper
in the dark parent bed, that dark
parent fear, "Will they like
our boy, our girl, our fine american
boy, our fine american girl?"[1]

1. Describe which ideas in the poem seem to be typically "American."

2. Why were Ruth's family "all trying to be American"?

3. Why would immigrants choose to do the things Pat Mora writes about?

4. Explain whether Pat Mora and Ruth McBride Jordan would agree with the statement that immigrants should not give up their cultural heritage for new beliefs and values.

[1]Pat Mora, "Immigrants," *Borders* (Houston: Arte Publico Press—University of Houston, 1986).

Name _____

Date _____

A Futile Fight

Directions: When have you found yourself fighting against injustices you can't name? When have you "stuffed" your feelings in order to avoid facing the truth? In prose or poetry, describe your own experiences.

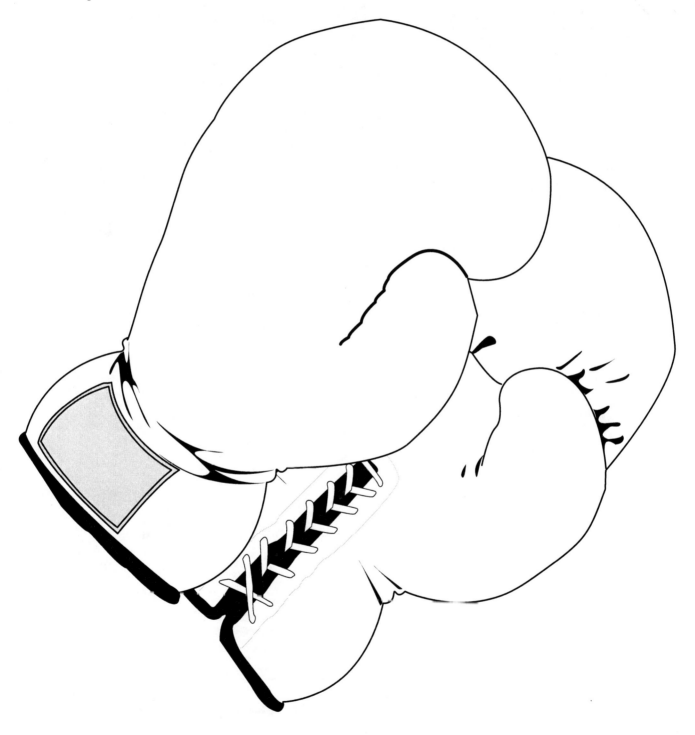

Great Expectations

Directions: James McBride's sister Jack tells him, "You have to choose between what the world expects of you and what you want for yourself." Address that advice in the organizer below.

What the world expects of me . . .	What I want for myself . . .

Is there a difference? If so, explain.

Do I see expectations as difficulties or opportunities?

How will I respond?

Lesson 7
Lost and Found

Objectives

- To understand connotation and denotation

- To appreciate McBride's characterizations

- To integrate character traits into a thumbnail sketch

Notes to the Teacher

To be lost is the great fear of every child. But is this a child's fear only? Or do adults experience it as well?

McBride answers these questions in chapters 17–20, the focus of Lesson 7. Through his feelings of loss and being lost and through his mother's experiences, we can examine ourselves and our own feelings about being lost. Lesson 7 will involve students in reviewing the way McBride emphasizes characterization, focusing in particular on chapters 2, 7, 8, and 20.

Procedure

1. Tell students to revisit their predictions for each chapter as delineated in Lesson 2, procedure 10. How accurate were their predictions? In what way(s) did they differ from McBride's story? Ask students to share these ideas with a partner.

2. Ask students to define the word *lost*. With a partner or small group, they should list scenarios in which people or things may be considered lost. These ideas can then be included in a class discussion.

3. Define *denotation*—the literal, dictionary definition of a word. Ask students if there are words with meanings other than the dictionary definitions. (*Students may mention slang terms such as cool, which can describe both a temperature and a person; or ghetto, which describes an inner-city slum area as well as an activity or attitude perceived as negative.*)

4. Point out that words with meanings other than a strict dictionary definition are intended as connotations which offer alternative, often symbolic, meanings.

5. Refer students to their ideas from procedure 2. Draw a T-chart on an overhead projector or chalkboard. Ask students to evaluate which of the scenarios they presented involve denotations of the word *lost* and which are connotations of that word.

6. Distribute **Handout 24**. Students may complete this individually, or you may wish to make an overhead transparency and complete it as a whole class activity.

7. Distribute **Handout 25**. Encourage students to draw on their responses from **Handout 24** in journaling James's and Ruth's experiences.

8. Refer to the quotations from **Handout 5** (Lesson 2) as students continue reading. Discuss which are applicable for their journals.

9. Have students write about a time when they have been lost, either literally or figuratively. This piece may be placed in students' portfolios and polished for later publication.

10. As a means of synthesizing chapters 17–20, distribute **Handout 26**, which can be used for homework or an in-class assignment.

Suggested Responses:

1. *Some problems that James might encounter are racism, segregation, poverty, the "hang-out crowd," and drugs.*

6. *Literally, Ruth had to sacrifice financially to send James to college; figuratively, she sacrificed his companionship by insisting that he go away to college, although she realized she would be sad.*

7. *Students may suggest that Ruth must deal with promises to her Tateh, Mameh, Bubeh, Dennis, and Dee-Dee.*

8. *So much of Ruth's past was negative that she may have been startled to tears by a kind voice. Additionally, Eddie Thompson's call may have reminded Ruth of events from her childhood better left forgotten.*

11. Review with students the methods that authors use to develop characters:

    - direct description by the author
    - the character's own words, thoughts, and/or actions
    - the responses of other characters to a particular character

12. Explore the descriptions of Mrs. Shilsky, Ruth's mother, and Mr. Shilsky, Ruth's father, offered by Eddie Thompson in chapter 20. Indicate the exchange McBride has with Thompson near the end of the chapter, where Thompson says, "The mother was crippled."

13. Distribute **Handout 27.** Have a student volunteer read the rest of chapter 20 to the class. As they read, students should complete part A by recording words or phrases that describe Ruth's parents, Mr. and Mrs. Shilsky. Review students' responses aloud.

    Suggested Responses:

Mrs. Shilsky	Mr. Shilsky
• *nice lady*	• *prejudiced*
• *would sneak fruit or candy*	• *cheated people*
• *crippled*	• *violent*
• *terrified of husband*	• *disliked by most*
• *caring*	• *hateful*

14. Direct students to complete part B of the exercise individually. They may share their responses with their classmates.

15. Assign part C of **Handout 27.** Emphasize that what students are to produce is a thumbnail sketch of someone they know well. Clarify that a thumbnail sketch is a very brief description of a person, similar to the ones Eddie Thompson offers at the end of chapter 20. Students' sketches should give a reader a sense of a person's character and physical appearance but should not go into great detail. (Part C may be used as the basis for a longer character study if desired.)

16. Assign chapters 21–24 in preparation for Lesson 8. Students should record a prediction based on each chapter's title in their journals.

Name _____

Date _____

Lost!

Directions: Use the chart to record how both James and Ruth are lost in chapters 17 and 18.

Connotations of the word *lost*	Denotations of the word *lost*

Name _____

Date _____

The Journals of Ruth and James

Directions: Chapters 17 and 18 present accounts of James's and his mother's being lost—in Harlem and in Delaware. Referring to those chapters, write journal entries as if you were James and Ruth, describing your feelings and actions.

Ruth (immediately upon arriving in New York)

Ruth (dealing with Aunt Mary)

Ruth (associating with Rocky)

James (awaiting Ruth's decision about moving)

James (dealing with the Delaware state troopers)

James (living in Wilmington)

Name _____

Date _____

Harlem, Delaware, and Points in Between

Directions: Read chapters 17–20, and answer the following questions.

1. List the problems that James might encounter when he moves to Wilmington.

2. In chapter 18, James refers to "the discipline of music" as a way of keeping him straight. How can extracurricular activities provide discipline for teenagers?

3. James confides in chapter 18 that his "anger at the world had been replaced by burning ambition." What does he mean?

4. According to James, "College was my way out." What does he mean by this statement? Is college the way out for everyone? Why or why not?

5. Predict how James's life might have been if not for college.

6. How was college a sacrifice for Ruth?

7. What are the promises in chapter 19 Ruth must deal with?

8. Analyze Ruth's reaction to the phone call from her past at the end of chapter 20.

Name _____

Date _____

Just a Sketch

Part A.

Directions: Record words or phrases from chapter 20 that describe Mr. and Mrs. Shilsky.

Mrs. Shilsky	Mr. Shilsky

Part B.

Directions: Make a chart as you did in part A, detailing words or phrases that describe your parents or others you know well.

Part C.

Directions: Using your ideas from part B, create a thumbnail sketch of one or both of the people you described.

Lesson 8
The American Dream

Objectives
• To interpret themes of the story

• To understand the concept of the American Dream

Notes to the Teacher
The American Dream is a theme that writers have explored for years. Nowhere is its exploration more poignant than in *The Color of Water*. Throughout McBride's book, we have seen how his mother survives hardships and endures trials that would have destroyed most people, all in her desire to achieve something lasting for herself and her family.

In addition, the author discovers things about himself that lead him to understand the American Dream as it applies to his own world. Through his introspection, we can determine for ourselves what our American Dreams are.

Previous lessons and objectives will continue to play a role in Lesson 8 as students delve into the themes in class discussion, add to their journals, and complete writing assignments.

Procedure
1. Assign students to create a Venn diagram, displaying similarities and differences between their predictions for chapters 21–24 and the events that McBride relates. Share these aloud.

2. Use the quotations from Lesson 2 as journal entries, discussion starters, or critical thinking activities as students progress through this lesson.

3. Recall with students the definition of symbolism, and ask students to explain the symbolism of the title of chapter 21, "A Bird Who Flies." (*Students may note that both Ruth and Mameh "fly" or escape.*)

4. In chapter 21, Ruth is cast out of the family because of her relationship with Dennis, an African-American man. In fact, her family considers her dead, and they sit shiva for her. Lead students in a discussion of how they would feel if they were effectively disowned by their families.

5. Ruth shows great courage and strength of character in chapter 21 when she decides to forgive her family after Mameh's death. Emphasize that Ruth must overcome her feelings about her father, who uses his hypocrisy as a weapon. Although Tateh is divorced from Ruth's mother, he uses Ruth's love for Mameh to try to make Ruth feel guilty enough to come home. Ruth must deal with the fact that although Tateh is a rabbi, he is also very prejudiced.

6. Distribute **Handout 28**. Any grammar or composition text will have sample letter formats that students may use as models for their own friendly letters. Because of the personal nature of this activity, students may wish to write this letter for their own portfolio.

7. In chapter 22, McBride gets in touch with a side of himself he had previously not known. In his introduction to this chapter, he writes that "Jewish holidays meant a day off from school . . . I certainly had no idea they had anything to do with me." However, after visiting his mother's childhood home in Suffolk, McBride realizes that Judaism was important to him after all.

8. Draw students' attention to the two Jewish holidays McBride mentions in the introduction to chapter 22. Invite students to define these holidays. Offer these definitions:

Rosh Hashana—the Jewish New Year, celebrated on the first and second days of the Jewish month of Tishri (falling in September or October). It begins the observance of the Ten Penitential Days, a period ending with Yom Kippur.

Yom Kippur—the most solemn and sacred holiday of the Jewish calendar. Yom Kippur is a day of confession, repentance, and prayers for forgiveness of sins committed during the year against God's laws and covenant. It is also the day on which an individual's fate for the ensuing year is thought to be sealed. Jews observe the day by a rigorous fast and nearly unbroken prayer.

9. Establish that although every religion has its own sacred holidays and traditions, those traditions need not be considered unrelated to others. From the ideas and values of other cultures, we can often learn something important for ourselves. Place students in pairs or small groups. Distribute **Handout 29**. It may be necessary to provide encyclopedias or Internet access for this research activity.

Suggested Responses:

Yom Kippur—a day of confession, repentance, and prayers for forgiveness of sins committed during the year against God's laws and covenant. This day of atonement could benefit me if I use it to spur me into asking forgiveness for wrongdoings.

Kwanzaa— the gathering of family, friends, and community; reverence for the creator and creation; commemoration of the past; recommitment to the highest cultural ideals of the African community; and celebration of life, struggle, achievement, family, community, and culture.

Christmas—in the Christian church, annual festival held on December 25 to celebrate the birth of Jesus Christ. Scholars believe that the festival is derived in part from rites held by pre-Christian Germanic and Celtic peoples to celebrate the winter solstice.

Ramadan—ninth month of the Islamic year, the holy month of fasting ordained by the Koran for all adult Muslims. According to the Koran, the fast has been instituted so that believers "may cultivate piety."

Hanukkah—commemorates the rededication to God of the Temple of Jerusalem by Judas Maccabee in 165 B.C.E., after it had been profaned by the worship of Zeus Olympius. According to tradition, only one small vessel of pure olive oil necessary for the rededicatory ritual could be found, but that quantity burned miraculously for eight days.

Las Posadas—Mexican Christmas festivities begin with Las Posadas, nine consecutive days of candlelight processions and lively parties starting December 16. Youngsters gather each afternoon to reenact the holy family's quest for lodging in Bethlehem.

Diwali, or Deepawali—a Hindu festival of lights symbolizing the victory of righteousness and the lifting of spiritual darkness. Twinkling oil lamps light up every home and firework displays are common all across the country. The goddess Lakshmi (consort of Vishnu), who is the symbol of wealth and prosperity, is also worshipped on this day. This festive occasion marks the beginning of the Hindu new year.

Chinese New Year—Nian, which in modern Chinese solely means *year*, was originally the name of a monster beast that started to prey on people the night before the beginning of the Chinese calendar's new year. Legend says that the beast would swallow a great many people with one bite. People were very frightened. One day, an old man came to their rescue, offering to subdue Nian. He said to Nian, "I hear say that you are very capable, but can you swallow the other beasts of prey on earth instead of people who are by no means your worthy opponents?" It did, and people began to enjoy their peaceful life. The old man told people to put up red paper decorations on their windows and doors at each year's end to scare away Nian in case it sneaked back again, because red is the color the beast feared the most.

10. Discuss McBride's thought from chapter 22 ". . . the greatest gift that anyone can give anyone else is life. And the greatest sin a person can do to another is to take away that life." Inquire of students who in *The Color of Water* had given life (both literally and figuratively), and who had taken away life. (*Ruth and her mother literally gave life through childbirth; figuratively, Ruth, Dennis, Hunter, and others who were kind gave life. Conversely, those like Tateh took away life through cruelty and racism.*)

11. Initiate a discussion of what dreams or goals students have for their futures. On an overhead projector or chalkboard, list these dreams and have students categorize them. (For example, some dreams may involve education; others may pertain to family.)

12. Continue the discussion of dreams by asking if students have ever heard of the phrase "the American Dream." Allow students to share definitions and/or examples. Propose to students that surely the American Dream is different for everyone. For some, it is wealth and power; for others, it is religious freedom and justice. For still more, it may be a roof over their heads.

13. Distribute **Handout 30,** part A to student pairs. Reinforce with students that achieving the American Dream may come at some cost, including sacrifices and overcoming obstacles. Ask students what attitudes, beliefs, and values helped Ruth achieve her dreams. Conduct a class discussion about students' responses.

14. Refer students to **Handout 30,** part B. It may be effective to model this activity for students. They should be given an extended amount of time to complete this research.

15. Distribute **Handout 31.** Students may keep this piece in their portfolios for further development and refinement.

16. Conclude a discussion of the American Dream with Dr. Martin Luther King, Jr.'s "I Have a Dream" speech on **Handout 32,** part A. Procure a recording or video of this famous speech for students, or invite students to prepare this speech for presentation to the class.

17. Instruct students to complete **Handout 32,** part B in small groups or pairs. Reinforce their learning by asking them to share their answers aloud.

    Suggested Responses:

    1. King may have been suggesting that he believes America will one day extend social and economic equality to all its citizens, regardless of race or religion.

    2. King comments on injustice and oppression; "vicious racists"; then-Governor George Wallace, who denied and nullified federal laws mandating equality. King does not blame; instead, he offers hope that these things will change.

    4. King's speech reflects the American Dream in that it calls for an end to inequality, which keeps people from achieving their goals. In addition, King espouses attitudes, beliefs, and values aligned to those of people who come to America seeking a chance to better themselves and their futures.

18. Direct students to read the remainder of the book in preparation for Lesson 9. Remind them to record predictions in their journal.

Optional Activities

1. Read the complete text of Dr. King's speech, available on the Internet at http://www.stanford.edu/group/King/Docs/march.html.

2. Prepare artwork depicting your understanding of the American Dream.

3. Study Lorraine Hansberry's classic drama about the American Dream, *A Raisin in the Sun.* Two outstanding films of this play are also available: the 1961 version starring Sidney Poitier, and the 1989 version starring Danny Glover.

4. Review chapter 24, and prepare the speech Ruth McBride Jordan gives at the fortieth anniversary gala in her honor. Make a presentation to the class.

Name _____

Date _____

Please, Mr. Postman

Directions: Is there someone to whom you—like Ruth McBride Jordan—should say "I'm sorry" or "I love you"? Write a letter doing so.

Name _____

Date _____

Celebrations

Directions: Use the chart to describe various religious holidays, traditions, and celebrations and how they may be applied to your own life.

Event	Description	Customs/Traditions	Application
Yom Kippur			
Kwanzaa			
Christmas			
Ramadan			
Hanukkah			
Las Posadas			
Diwali			
Chinese New Year			

The Color of Water
Lesson 8
Handout 20 (page 1)

Name _____

Date _____

Dream On

Part A.

Directions: Using the compartment organizer, reflect on the American Dream that Ruth McBride Jordan had for herself and her family.

Dreams

Obstacles	Strategies

Beliefs

Attitudes

Values

Name _____

Date _____

Part B.

Directions: Interview family members or friends of your family to determine what American Dreams others have held. Complete the compartment organizer.

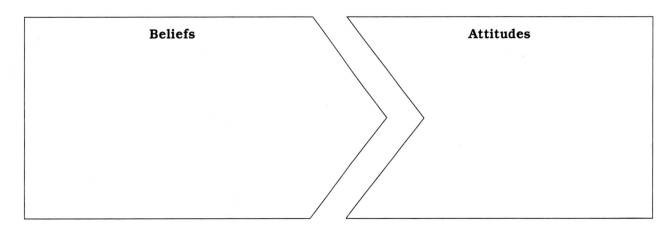

Name _____

Date _____

I Must Be Dreaming

Directions: In a well-written composition, describe your own American Dream. What obstacles might you need to overcome? What strategies can you use to overcome them? What attitudes, beliefs, and values will help you achieve your dream?

"I Have a Dream"

Part A.

Directions: Read this excerpt from Dr. Martin Luther King, Jr.'s famous speech from the steps of the Lincoln Memorial in Washington, D.C., August 28, 1963.

So, I say to you, my friends, that even though we must face the difficulties of today and tomorrow, I still have a dream. It is a dream deeply rooted in the American dream that one day this nation will rise up and live out the true meaning of its creed—we hold these truths to be self-evident, that all men are created equal.

I have a dream that one day on the red hills of Georgia, sons of former slaves and sons of former slaveowners will be able to sit down together at a table of brotherhood.

I have a dream that one day, even the state of Mississippi, a state sweltering with the heat of injustice, sweltering with the heat of oppression, will be transformed into an oasis of freedom and justice.

I have a dream that my four little children will one day live in a nation where they will not be judged by the color of their skin but by the content of their character. I have a dream today!

I have a dream that one day, down in Alabama with its vicious racists, with its governor having his lips dripping with the words of interposition and nullification, that one day, right there in Alabama, little black boys and black girls will be able to join hands with little white boys and white girls and walk together as sisters and brothers. I have a dream today!

I have a dream that one day every valley shall be exalted, every hill and mountain shall be made low, the rough places will be made plain, and the crooked places will be made straight and the glory of the Lord shall be revealed and all flesh shall see it together.

This is our hope. This is the faith that I return to the South with.

With this faith we will be able to hew out of the mountain of despair a stone of hope. With this faith we will be able to transform the jangling discords of our nation into a beautiful symphony of brotherhood.

With this faith we will be able to work together, to pray together, to struggle together, to go to jail together, to stand up for freedom together, knowing that we will be free one day. This will be the day when all of God's children will be able to sing with a new meaning—"my country, 'tis of thee; sweet land of liberty; of thee I sing; land where my fathers died, land of the pilgrim's pride; from every mountain side, let freedom ring"—and if America is to be a great nation this must become true.

So let freedom ring from the prodigious hilltops of New Hampshire.

Let freedom ring from the mighty mountains of New York.

Let freedom ring from the heightening Alleghenies of Pennsylvania.

Let freedom ring from the snowcapped Rockies of Colorado.

Let freedom ring from the curvaceous peaks of California.

But not only that.

Let freedom ring from Stone Mountain of Georgia.

Let freedom ring from Lookout Mountain of Tennessee.

Let freedom ring from every hill and every molehill of Mississippi, from every mountainside, let freedom ring.

And when we let freedom ring, when we let it ring from every village and hamlet, from every state and city, we will be able to speed up that day when all of God's children—black men and white men, Jews and Gentiles, Catholics and Protestants—will be able to join hands and sing in the words of the old Negro spiritual, "Free at last, free at last, thank God Almighty, we are free at last."[2]

Part B.

Directions: Answer these questions about Dr. King's speech.

1. What does King mean when he says he dreams that the United States will "live out the true meaning of its creed"?

2. What were Martin Luther King, Jr.,'s criticisms of American society?

3. What portions of King's speech would resonate most with Ruth McBride Jordan?

4. How does King's speech reflect the American Dream?

[1]Martin Luther King, Jr., "I Have a Dream," *Negro History Bulletin* 21 (May 1968): 16–17. In *A Testament of Hope: The Essential Writings and Speeches of Martin Luther King, Jr.,* ed. James M. Washington (New York: HarperCollins Publishers, 1986), 219–220.

Lesson 9
Self Discovered

Objectives

- To integrate McBride's experiences into personal experience

- To highlight the theme of identity

Notes to the Teacher

Throughout this memoir/biography, James McBride has looked for an identity. The irony is that until he found his mother, he was unable to find himself. In this lesson, students will use McBride's experiences to develop their own strategies for finding themselves.

Procedure

1. Ask students to share their predictions for chapter 25 and the Epilogue.

2. With the class, review Ruth's account of her life with Dennis in chapter 23. Review with students the hardships and sacrifices both Ruth and Dennis endured. Despite these difficulties, Ruth states that her "soul was full." Suggest that Ruth felt satisfied with her life because she was comfortable with who she was.

3. Ask students to describe what being comfortable with themselves might mean. Lead students to an understanding that being comfortable with oneself means knowing who one is, what one stands for, what one's value is to others, what one's purpose is in life. Knowing these things, Ruth could say that her "soul was full."

4. After students have read chapters 1–24, ask whether they believe McBride is comfortable with who he is. Students must cite textual examples to support their opinions.

5. Distribute **Handout 33**. Complete it as a class. (*Students may offer that characteristics such as race, gender, dress, sexual orientation, convictions, and peer group can all make statements about people. They may note that stereotyping, previous experiences, the media, and lack of education all play a part in people's making assumptions about others.*)

6. Continue this discussion by posing the following questions to the class: Is making such assumptions about others good or bad? Why? How can we get beyond such assumptions when dealing with others? Invite students to discuss their personal experiences with assumptions such as these.

7. Refer to the quotations from Lesson 2 in students' journals as they work through this lesson.

8. Engage students in a discussion and review of Ruth's beliefs from **Handout 9**. Stress that those beliefs were passed on to her children, and that her strong beliefs influenced each one of them.

9. Distribute **Handout 34**. Students may work in small groups or pairs. Answers can be found near the end of Chapter 25, where McBride lists his and his siblings' accomplishments.

   In pairs or small groups, have students trace the events that may have influenced the lives of Ruth McBride Jordan's twelve children. Student answers will vary but must be supported with examples from the text.

10. Point out that after coming to terms with his race and identity, McBride undergoes a maturation even as an adult. He becomes comfortable with himself, with his mother, with his past.

11. Explain that author John O'Neil has written a book called *Leadership Aikido: 6 Business Practices to Turn around Your Life*. In this book, he discusses the Asian combat art *aikido*, whose purpose is to bring conflict to a harmonious conclusion without ever harming the aggressor. O'Neil maintains that high achievers in any field can use the principles of this ancient art to overcome the "Five Inner Enemies"—failing to grow emotionally, failing to make creative connections, failing to empathize, failing to manage ego, and failing to overcome alienation and boredom.[1] Remind

[1] John O'Neil, *Leadership Aikido: 6 Business Practices to Turn Around Your Life* (New York: Harmony Books, 1997), 11.

students that these Five Inner Enemies play roles in McBride's story. Without conquering them, McBride and his siblings would never have achieved their—or their mother's—goals.

12. Distribute **Handout 35**. Since part A is a whole-book review activity, it may be most effective for students to work in pairs or small groups. Although students' responses will vary, their answers must be supported with textual examples.

13. Assign **Handout 35,** part B. This writing may be in prose or poetry form. Specify the criteria for a well-written composition before students begin writing. This reflective piece may be kept in students' portfolios for further refinement.

14. Request that students choose one of the five enemies that McBride faced in *The Color of Water*. Ask them to rewrite that situation, with the outcome being different from what actually happened to McBride. Allow students to share these rewrites with other class members.

Optional Activities

1. Role-play any of the scenarios you rewrote in procedure 14.

2. Rehearse your prose or poetry compositions from **Handout 35,** and present them to the class.

Name _____

Date _____

Positive ID

Part A.

Directions: In chapter 25, McBride tells us that " . . . the color of your face [is] an immediate political statement whether you like it or not." Do other identifying characteristics seem to make a statement about people?

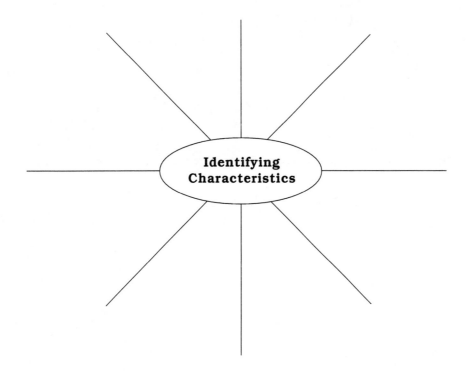

Part B.

Directions: List what causes people to make assumptions about others based on the characteristics you listed above.

Name _____

Date _____

Success by the Dozen

Directions: Remarkably, all twelve children of Ruth McBride Jordan—children who grew up amid poverty and hardship—succeeded despite the odds. List the successes of Ruth's children.

1. Andrew D. McBride

2. Rosetta McBride

3. William McBride

4. David McBride

5. Helen McBride-Richter

6. Richard McBride

7. Dorothy R. McBride-Wesley

8. James C. McBride

9. Kathy L. Jordan

10. Judy D. Jordan

11. Hunter L. Jordan

12. Henry Jordan

Name _____

Date _____

The Five Inner Enemies

Part A.

Directions: Review the difficulties that James McBride experienced throughout his life. Record an instance of McBride's facing these inner enemies, and describe how he overcame each of the five inner enemies that could have ruined him.

Inner Enemy	Facing Enemies	Overcoming Enemies
Failing to grow emotionally		
Failing to make creative connections		
Failing to empathize		
Failing to manage ego		
Failing to overcome alienation and boredom[2]		

Part B.

Directions: Look at your own life. In a well-written composition, discuss times when you have faced any of the five inner enemies. Describe your failure or success in overcoming these enemies.

[2]John O'Neil, *Leadership Aikido: 6 Business Practices to Turn Around Your Life* (New York: Harmony Books, 1997), 11.

Lesson 10
Tell It Like It Was

Objectives
- To conduct an oral history interview

- To write a memoir

Notes to the Teacher
What a treasure we have in the stories of our parents and grandparents, our aunts and uncles, our ancestors who come to this country! Certainly their stories and experiences teach us invaluable lessons about suffering separation and endurance. Their memories open up history for us in ways that no textbook ever could.

The Color of Water is a remarkable example of how the oral history of Ruth McBride Jordan enriches the lives of all who hear it. We are able to live life as she lived it, to experience the hardships that she experienced, and to feel the joys and sorrows she felt. Emphasizing the importance of oral history to our society is integral to this lesson, as students will have the opportunity to interview someone and write a memoir.

Procedure
1. Ask students to describe what comes to mind when they think of *history*. Pose this question to students: Would you rather read a chapter in a history text about the Holocaust, or would you rather speak to someone who lived through it? Have students explain their reasons aloud.

2. Remind students that *The Color of Water* presents historical events through the eyes of both McBride and his mother. Although not strictly limited to documented history that students might study in school, the author's recollections and those of his mother do reflect historical experiences that many other people understand.

3. Check that students understand that the foremost value of oral history is its pertinence to social history, allowing us to reconstruct "the fabric of daily life since the turn of the century. . . [and to document] the mundane details of family and community life . . .", as one oral historian put it.

4. Use an overhead projector or chalkboard to discuss the types of people who would make good oral historians, people who could contribute details about everyday life in another time period or another country. (*Students may list people such as grandparents or other family members, teachers, residents of retirement complexes, members of senior citizens' centers, members of the clergy, neighbors, recent immigrants, politicians, or members of philanthropic groups such as the Lions or Kiwanis.*)

5. Query students as to what possible topics they would want to discuss if they were to interview any of the individuals listed in procedure 4. (Students might list careers; family life; life for women, minorities, or teenagers; war or military experiences; or journeys made by immigrants as possible topics.)

6. Distribute **Handout 36**. Review these tips with students, and encourage them to keep the tips handy as they prepare for and conduct their interviews.

7. Assign students the task of writing the questions they will use in their interviews. Allow students to rehearse these questions in pairs.

8. Because of the extended nature of this assignment, create a time line with students that reflects your expectations for the timely completion of this project. A sample is provided on **Handout 37**; modifications may be made to this as needed.

9. Allot class time as necessary according to your time line for students to work on the organization and rough drafts of their memoirs.

10. To give closure to this unit, have students review the thanks and acknowledgments McBride includes at the end of *The Color of Water*. Mention that each of the people McBride lists has in some way helped him in his journey through life.

11. Examine **Handout 38** with students. Model for them your own acknowledgments; stress that their work does not need to be as lengthy as McBride's. Invite them to share these thanks and acknowledgments with those people they mention, if possible.

Optional Activity

Present your completed memoirs to the class.

Name _____

Date _____

Tips for Interview Success

Directions: Refer to this sheet as you plan and conduct your oral history interviews.

Pre-Interview Guidelines

1. When contacting the prospective interviewee, clearly present your purpose. Indicate how much time will be involved and what general areas will be covered.

2. Ask permission to tape record your interview sessions, but be prepared to take notes if the interviewee is uncomfortable being recorded.

3. Do enough background reading or research to have some idea of the time period about which you will question the interviewee.

4. Write a question outline that you will use to guide the interview. Include biographical questions as well as questions that may lead the interviewee into discussing other issues. You may share this question outline with the interviewee in advance of the actual interview to stimulate his or her memories.

5. Set the location of the interview in a quiet place where you won't be disturbed. Familiar territory such as the interviewee's home may enhance the session. Telephone the day before the interview to remind the person of your appointment.

Interview Technique Guidelines

1. Ask open-ended questions, not those inviting a *yes* or *no* response. For example, a question such as "How did the Depression affect your family?" is much better than "Did the Depression affect your family?"

2. Allow the interviewee to answer your questions freely, without interrupting him or her. However, if he or she begins to wander, interject with a statement such as "Your memories have brought many topics to mind that I'd like to know more about. Could you tell me about _____?"

3. Listen very carefully, jotting down notes for further questions.

4. Establish eye contact when appropriate to convey your interest.

5. Don't be afraid to ask clarifying questions if you don't understand something the interviewee has said.

6. At the conclusion of the interview, thank the interviewee for his or her time. Assure him or her that you will call if you have any further questions, and encourage the interviewee to call you if he or she has more information that will be helpful.

Name _____

Date _____ _____

On This Day in History . . .

Directions: Use the following time line to check your progress on this project.

Day 1	Day 2	Day 7	Day 8	Day 9	Day 12
Create interview questions	Arrange for interview	Conduct interview	Organize interview information	Write rough draft of memoir	Submit final draft of memoir

Day 1	Day 2	Day 7	Day 8	Day 9	Day 12

Name _____

Date _____

Thanks for the Memories

Directions: If you were the author of a book about your life or your family's life, whom would you thank? What acknowledgments would you give for lessons learned?

Bibliography

Aguilera, Charity. Personal Interview. 3 March 1999.

American Life Histories: Manuscripts from the Federal Writers' Project, 1936–1940. Available online: http://lcweb2.loc.gov/wpaintro/wpahome.html

Hughes, Langston. "Theme for English B." *Montage of a Dream Deferred.* New York: Henry Holt, 1951.

McBride, James. *The Color of Water: A Black Man's Tribute to His White Mother.* Dove Books Audio: February 1996.

Mora, Pat. "Immigrants." *Borders.* Houston: Arte Publico Press—University of Houston, 1986.

Narrative of the Life of Frederick Douglass, An American Slave. Available online: http://www.americanliterature.com/NARR/NARRINDX.HTML

Student oral history projects. http://www.teci.net/bland/rocky/gap.html

Washington, James M., ed. *A Testament of Hope: The Essential Writings and Speeches of Martin Luther King, Jr.* New York: Harper Collins, 1986.

Acknowledgments

For permission to reprint all works in this volume, grateful acknowledgment is made to the following holders of copyright, publishers, or representatives.

Lesson 1, Handout 9

Scripture quotation is from the New Revised Standard Version Bible, copyright © 1989 by the Division of Christian Education of the National Council of the Churches of Christ in the U.S.A., and is used by permission. All rights reserved.

Lesson 5, Handout 17

For use of "Theme for English B" from *Collected Poems* by Langston Hughes. Copyright © 1994 by the Estate of Langston Hughes. Reprinted by permission of Alfred A. Knopf, Inc.

Lesson 6, Handout 23

"Immigrants" by Pat Mora is reprinted with permission from the publisher of *Borders* (Houston: Arte Publico Press—University of Houston, 1986).

Lesson 8, Handout 32

For use of excerpt from the "I Have a Dream" speech by Martin Luther King, Jr. Copyright 1963 by Martin Luther King, Jr., copyright renewed 1991 by Coretta Scott King. Reprinted with permission.

NOVEL / DRAMA

CURRICULUM UNITS

Novel/Drama Series

Novel

*Absolutely Normal Chaos/
    Chasing Redbird*, Creech

Across Five Aprils, Hunt

Adam of the Road, Gray/*Catherine,
    Called Birdy*, Cushman

*The Adventures of Huckleberry
    Finn*, Twain

The Adventures of Tom Sawyer,
    Twain

*Alice's Adventures in Wonderland/
    Through the Looking-Glass*,
    Carroll

All Creatures Great and Small,
    Herriot

All Quiet on the Western Front,
    Remarque

All the King's Men, Warren

Animal Farm, Orwell/
    The Book of the Dun Cow,
    Wangerin, Jr.

Anna Karenina, Tolstoy

*Anne Frank: The Diary of a Young
    Girl*, Frank

Anne of Green Gables, Montgomery

April Morning, Fast

The Assistant/The Fixer, Malamud

*The Autobiography of Miss Jane
    Pittman*, Gaines

The Awakening, Chopin/
    Madame Bovary, Flaubert

Babbitt, Lewis

The Bean Trees/Pigs in Heaven,
    Kingsolver

Beowulf/Grendel, Gardner

Billy Budd/Moby Dick, Melville

Black Boy, Wright

Bless Me, Ultima, Anaya

Brave New World, Huxley

The Bridge of San Luis Rey, Wilder

The Brothers Karamazov,
    Dostoevsky

The Call of the Wild/White Fang,
    London

The Canterbury Tales, Chaucer

The Catcher in the Rye, Salinger

The Cay/Timothy of the Cay, Taylor

Charlotte's Web, White/
    The Secret Garden, Burnett

The Chosen, Potok

The Christmas Box, Evans/
    A Christmas Carol, Dickens

Chronicles of Narnia, Lewis

Cold Sassy Tree, Burns

*The Color of Water: A Black Man's
    Tribute to His White Mother*,
    McBride

The Count of Monte Cristo, Dumas

Crime and Punishment, Dostoevsky

Cry, the Beloved Country, Paton

Dandelion Wine, Bradbury

Darkness at Noon, Koestler

David Copperfield, Dickens

Davita's Harp, Potok

A Day No Pigs Would Die, Peck

Death Comes for the Archbishop,
    Cather

December Stillness, Hahn/
    Izzy, Willy-Nilly, Voigt

The Divine Comedy, Dante

The Dollmaker, Arnow

Don Quixote, Cervantes

Dr. Zhivago, Pasternak

Dubliners, Joyce

East of Eden, Steinbeck

The Egypt Game, Snyder/
    The Bronze Bow, Speare

Ellen Foster/A Virtuous Woman,
    Gibbons

Emma, Austen

Fahrenheit 451, Bradbury

A Farewell to Arms, Hemingway

Farewell to Manzanar, Houston &
    Houston/*Black Like Me*, Griffin

Frankenstein, Shelley

*From the Mixed-up Files of Mrs.
    Basil E. Frankweiler*,
    Konigsburg/*The Westing Game*,
    Raskin

A Gathering of Flowers, Thomas, ed.

The Giver, Lowry

The Good Earth, Buck

The Grapes of Wrath, Steinbeck

Great Expectations, Dickens

The Great Gatsby, Fitzgerald

Gulliver's Travels, Swift

Hard Times, Dickens

Hatchet, Paulsen/*Robinson Crusoe*,
    Defoe

Having Our Say, Delany, Delany,
    and Hearth/
    A Gathering of Old Men, Gaines

The Heart Is a Lonely Hunter,
    McCullers

Heart of Darkness, Conrad

Hiroshima, Hersey/*On the Beach*,
    Shute

The Hobbit, Tolkien

Homecoming/Dicey's Song, Voigt

The Hound of the Baskervilles,
    Doyle

*The Human Comedy/
    My Name Is Aram*, Saroyan

Incident at Hawk's Hill, Eckert/
    Where the Red Fern Grows,
    Rawls

Invisible Man, Ellison

Jane Eyre, Brontë

Johnny Tremain, Forbes

Journey of the Sparrows, Buss and
    Cubias/*The Honorable Prison*, de
    Jenkins

The Joy Luck Club, Tan

Jubal Sackett/The Walking Drum,
    L'Amour

Julie of the Wolves, George/*Island
    of the Blue Dolphins*, O'Dell

The Jungle, Sinclair

The Killer Angels, Shaara

Le Morte D'Arthur, Malory

The Learning Tree, Parks

Les Miserables, Hugo

*The Light in the Forest/
    A Country of Strangers*, Richter

*Little House in the Big Woods/
    Little House on the Prairie*,
    Wilder

Little Women, Alcott

Lord of the Flies, Golding

The Lord of the Rings, Tolkien

The Martian Chronicles, Bradbury

Missing May, Rylant/*The Summer
    of the Swans*, Byars

Mrs. Mike, Freedman/*I Heard the
    Owl Call My Name*, Craven

*Murder on the Orient Express/
    And Then There Were None*,
    Christie

My Antonia, Cather

The Natural, Malamud/*Shoeless
    Joe*, Kinsella

Nectar in a Sieve, Markandaya/
    The Woman Warrior, Kingston

Night, Wiesel

A Night to Remember, Lord/
    *Streams to the River, River to the
    Sea*, O'Dell

1984, Orwell

Number the Stars, Lowry/*Friedrich*,
    Richter

Obasan, Kogawa

The Odyssey, Homer

The Old Man and the Sea,
    Hemingway/*Ethan Frome*,
    Wharton

The Once and Future King, White

O Pioneers!, Cather/*The Country of the Pointed Firs*, Jewett

Ordinary People, Guest/ *The Tin Can Tree*, Tyler

The Outsiders, Hinton/ *Durango Street*, Bonham

The Pearl/Of Mice and Men, Steinbeck

The Picture of Dorian Gray, Wilde/ *Dr. Jekyll and Mr. Hyde*, Stevenson

The Pigman/The Pigman's Legacy, Zindel

A Portrait of the Artist as a Young Man, Joyce

The Power and the Glory, Greene

A Prayer for Owen Meany, Irving

Pride and Prejudice, Austen

The Prince, Machiavelli/*Utopia*, More

The Prince and the Pauper, Twain

Profiles in Courage, Kennedy

Rebecca, du Maurier

The Red Badge of Courage, Crane

Red Sky at Morning, Bradford

The Return of the Native, Hardy

A River Runs Through It, Maclean

Roll of Thunder, Hear My Cry/ Let the Circle Be Unbroken, Taylor

Saint Maybe, Tyler

Sarum, Rutherfurd

The Scarlet Letter, Hawthorne

The Scarlet Pimpernel, Orczy

A Separate Peace, Knowles

Shabanu: Daughter of the Wind/ Haveli, Staples

Shane, Schaefer/*The Ox-Bow Incident*, Van Tilburg Clark

Siddhartha, Hesse

The Sign of the Chrysanthemum/ The Master Puppeteer, Paterson

The Signet Classic Book of Southern Short Stories, Abbott and Koppelman, eds.

Silas Marner, Eliot/ *The Elephant Man*, Sparks

The Slave Dancer, Fox/ *I, Juan de Pareja*, De Treviño

Snow Falling on Cedars, Guterson

Song of Solomon, Morrison

The Sound and the Fury, Faulkner

Spoon River Anthology, Masters

A Stranger Is Watching/I'll Be Seeing You, Higgins Clark

The Stranger/The Plague, Camus

Summer of My German Soldier, Greene/*Waiting for the Rain*, Gordon

A Tale of Two Cities, Dickens

Talking God/A Thief of Time, Hillerman

Tess of the D'Urbervilles, Hardy

Their Eyes Were Watching God, Hurston

Things Fall Apart/No Longer at Ease, Achebe

To Kill a Mockingbird, Lee

To the Lighthouse, Woolf

Travels with Charley, Steinbeck

Treasure Island, Stevenson

A Tree Grows in Brooklyn, Smith

Tuck Everlasting, Babbitt/ *Bridge to Terabithia*, Paterson

The Turn of the Screw/Daisy Miller, James

Uncle Tom's Cabin, Stowe

Walden, Thoreau/*A Different Drummer*, Kelley

Walk Two Moons, Creech

Walkabout, Marshall

Watership Down, Adams

The Watsons Go to Birmingham— 1963, Curtis/*The View from Saturday*, Konigsburg

When the Legends Die, Borland

Where the Lilies Bloom, Cleaver/ *No Promises in the Wind*, Hunt

Winesburg, Ohio, Anderson

The Witch of Blackbird Pond, Speare/*My Brother Sam Is Dead*, Collier and Collier

A Wrinkle in Time, L'Engle/*The Lion, the Witch and the Wardrobe*, Lewis

Wuthering Heights, Brontë

The Yearling, Rawlings/ *The Red Pony*, Steinbeck

Year of Impossible Goodbyes, Choi/ *So Far from the Bamboo Grove*, Watkins

Zlata's Diary, Filipović/ *The Lottery Rose*, Hunt

Drama

Antigone, Sophocles

Arms and the Man/Saint Joan, Shaw

The Crucible, Miller

Cyrano de Bergerac, Rostand

Death of a Salesman, Miller

A Doll's House/Hedda Gabler, Ibsen

The Glass Menagerie, Williams

The Importance of Being Earnest, Wilde

Inherit the Wind, Lawrence and Lee

Long Day's Journey into Night, O'Neill

A Man for All Seasons, Bolt

Medea, Euripides/*The Lion in Winter*, Goldman

The Miracle Worker, Gibson

Murder in the Cathedral, Eliot/ *Galileo*, Brecht

The Night Thoreau Spent in Jail, Lawrence and Lee

Oedipus the King, Sophocles

Our Town, Wilder

The Playboy of the Western World/ Riders to the Sea, Synge

Pygmalion, Shaw

A Raisin in the Sun, Hansberry

1776, Stone and Edwards

She Stoops to Conquer, Goldsmith/ *The Matchmaker*, Wilder

A Streetcar Named Desire, Williams

Tartuffe, Molière

Three Comedies of American Family Life: I Remember Mama, van Druten/*Life with Father*, Lindsay and Crouse/*You Can't Take It with You*, Hart and Kaufman

Waiting for Godot, Beckett/ *Rosencrantz & Guildenstern Are Dead*, Stoppard

Shakespeare

As You Like It

Hamlet

Henry IV, Part I

Henry V

Julius Caesar

King Lear

Macbeth

The Merchant of Venice

A Midsummer Night's Dream

Much Ado about Nothing

Othello

Richard III

Romeo and Juliet

The Taming of the Shrew

The Tempest

Twelfth Night

The Center for Learning

To Order Contact: **The Center for Learning—Shipping/Business Office**
P.O. Box 910 • Villa Maria, PA 16155
800-767-9090 • 724-964-8083 • Fax 888-767-8080

The Publisher

All instructional materials identified by the TAP® (Teachers/Authors/Publishers) trademark are developed by a national network of teachers whose collective educational experience distinguishes the publishing objective of The Center for Learning, a nonprofit educational corporation founded in 1970.

Concentrating on values-related disciplines, the Center publishes humanities and religion curriculum units for use in public and private schools and other educational settings. Approximately 500 language arts, social studies, novel/drama, life issues, and faith publications are available.

While acutely aware of the challenges and uncertain solutions to growing educational problems, the Center is committed to quality curriculum development and to the expansion of learning opportunities for all students. Publications are regularly evaluated and updated to meet the changing and diverse needs of teachers and students. Teachers may offer suggestions for development of new publications or revisions of existing titles by contacting

The Center for Learning

Administrative/Editorial Office
21590 Center Ridge Road
Rocky River, OH 44116
(440) 331-1404 • FAX (440) 331-5414
E-mail: cfl@stratos.net
Web: www.centerforlearning.org

For a free catalog containing order and price information and a descriptive listing of titles, contact

The Center for Learning

Shipping/Business Office
P.O. Box 910
Villa Maria, PA 16155
(724) 964-8083 • (800) 767-9090
FAX (888) 767-8080